BATHROOM REMODELING

DESIGNING YOUR PERFECT BATHROOM WITH AN ARCHITECT

RENOVATE YOUR BATHROOM NOW!

By Amy Landri

TABLE OF CONTENTS

WHERE TO START

Usually, the first thoughts that come to us, thinking about how to renovate a bathroom are which tiles are in fashion; are the countertop or sanitary ware better; the floor-level shower is what makes my bathroom a special thing; hydromassage would be the best ... you could read some specialized magazines that can advise you on the latest fashions and trends, but you will not find anything that explains the practical aspects, such as planning how to create a bathroom. Which are the main aspects you should take care of as soon as you decide to renovate your bathroom.

The reasons, before thinking about the aesthetic part, that it is important to think about all the practical aspects are very simple:

The company to which you entrust the work may know less than you about the practices necessary to do the work without illegalities or about which state incentives to use, perhaps taking many fundamental things for granted, in order to finish the work immediately and quickly.

So, these are the things you need to know for a perfect bathroom renovation:

✓ All the problems you will face
✓ The layout of the sanitary ware and the minimum distances
✓ The finishes you can choose from
✓ How much, at the end of the day, it will cost you to redo the bathroom

So, what does it really mean to renovate a bathroom?

This aspect is really important if we do not want to fall into the hands of someone who offers us cheap and hasty solutions. If you think that the renovation of the bathroom means only changing the bathroom fixtures, moving them or changing the arrangement because we are tired of seeing them like this for too many years and replacing the old tiles, perhaps with something more modern, we are on the wrong path.

The next question is why did you decide to renovate the bathroom?

The most immediate answer is: the bathroom is now old and the tiles are ugly and the joints are black with mold, the toilet is encrusted and clogs up, the tub is ruined and does not give me that sense of well-being when I immerse myself in it, the mirror is falling off the wall and the taps risk coming off in my hand or I have to struggle to open them. These are the considerations that you can make with the naked eye and that make you evaluate the idea that perhaps the time has come to redo your bathroom. Think carefully if they are to change the suite and taps, will you also want to change everything that is unseen?

The fundamental parts of a bathroom are mostly hidden: the functional parts, you do not see them because they are under the plaster or under the floor, but they are essential and a source of serious problems if deteriorated or malfunctioning. But, just as the faucets and the shower get worn out or clogged, the drain pipes of the sink, the pipes, the wells, wear out over time, and end up breaking and can cause flooding that can ruin the various floors of the house or the building with thousands of dollars in damages and compensation.

So, the replacement of the finishes is only an aesthetic touch-up for your bathroom while the probable problems due to the wear of the pipes will remain unsolved.

Is it worth doing an economic and purely aesthetic restyling with the risk of having to dismantle everything and break all the tiles, perhaps after a short time, due to a loss that forces you to redo all the systems?

THE REAL PROBLEMS YOU WILL HAVE TO TACKLE IN A BATHROOM RENOVATION

The time has come to talk about the practical problems (or if you want to call them also, technical) that will surely emerge during the work, but that you can very well foresee before they start! No business and often not even the technicians will tell you about it until it is time to face them ... but you can avoid arriving unprepared. I want to reassure you: it is nothing dramatic and unsolvable, but if not taken into due consideration from the early stages they could give you unpleasant surprises (also and above all economically).

Problem 1: how much screed do you have under the floor?

    You've probably happened to walk into some recently remodeled bathroom inside a 30/40-year-old condominium. One thing you have surely noticed is that, somewhere, there is a step that divides the bathroom into two parts: one higher and one lower. This is by no means an aesthetic solution expressly desired by the client (although objectively, almost always the effect is beautiful) but simply a solution adopted to solve a technical problem: the lack of sufficient space under the tiles to be able to pass the pipes of the installations.

    Let's try to understand: all the sanitary fittings in your bathroom are connected both to a water supply line (hot and cold) and to a water discharge line towards the sewer. This second line must converge towards what are commonly called drainpipes: vertical ducts that convey all the waste water from the apartments of a condominium to the municipal sewer. Try to find it: probably in your bathroom, perhaps near the window, there is an enlargement of the wall, as if it were a column: that is not a supporting column but a duct through which the pipe that collects all the drains of the apartments. Your bathroom must also direct all the waste water from the sink, bidet, toilet, shower / tub to that pipe. And to do this, pipes are put under the floor.

The waste water discharge system works by gravity: that is, they go from top to bottom (unlike the water supply system which works by pressure). Therefore, to make sure that everything works correctly without the risk of it becoming clogged every day, the part of the plant responsible for disposal cannot be perfectly level but must have a minimum slope. Basically, the pipes you have under the floor cannot be perfectly horizontal but must be slightly inclined.

Furthermore, to ensure a better functionality of the whole system, the drains of the sanitary appliances (with the exception of the toilet) are conveyed to a small circular well which can be accessed in the event that some object accidentally ends up in the drain (how many rings have been saved from these wells?), or for any other type of obstruction / damage, simplifying and making all maintenance operations much cheaper. Starting from this well, a tube, which of course must always be sloping, enters the drain column.

Why is the toilet not inserted in this pit?

The pipe that comes out of the toilet has a larger diameter than the one that comes out of the other sanitary ware, I think it's easy to imagine why.

Therefore, it is not convenient to convey it to a well together with the other drains, but it is much more practical to introduce it directly into the drain.

This whole set of systems consisting of pipes and pit is always positioned on the floor and, at its thickest point, usually reaches up to 15 centimeters high. And here the problem arises: all the buildings built up to no more than 20 years ago have always provided for screeds with a thickness much less than 15 centimeters (in reality, even new ones rarely reach these thicknesses). And the further back you go in time (so the older the building in which the bathroom is to be restored) the more the thickness of the screeds decreases, to arrive at thicknesses equal to the minimum necessary to lay the floor (we are talking about only 3-4 cm). So, in these cases (and if your bathroom to be restored is in a building with at least thirty years of life) in order to create a system that works well and that will not give you problems over time, you will almost certainly have to provide a step inside your bathroom.

The most common solution is to keep the part of the bathroom with the sink at the same height as the rest of the house, while the part with all the other sanitary fittings (bidet, toilet, shower / tub) is raised.

Of course, this does not have to happen always and necessarily: a lot depends on when and how your property was built, but it is a probability that you must take into consideration.

In terms of costs, it does not very much, it is a matter of a few centimeters of light concrete, but it varies a lot in terms

of aesthetics. And, I have to tell you again: dividing the bathroom into a low area and a high area often makes your bathroom much more beautiful. So, a technical necessity that translates into an aesthetic improvement.

Problem 2: is the wall thick enough?

WC with External Cassette

I know it sounds like an absurd question but stay with me. Does the toilet you currently have in the bathroom have the drain pan positioned at the top? Or is it positioned in sight just behind the toilet? If the answer is yes, the wall on which it is fixed is probably not thick enough to allow the installation of a recessed box.

In fact, among all the systems that are embedded in the walls that line the bathroom, the basin containing the waste water is the element with the greatest thickness.

This basin is actually not very thick, usually around 10 centimeters (now even a bit less) but many years ago it was common to build the walls of the bathroom with 8-centimeter-thick bricks to which two layers of plaster were added to get to a thickness overall of about 11cm. You understand that in such a small thickness it is not possible to insert a concealed cistern if not risking that in the next room a lump will appear at the height of the toilet cistern!

So how to solve the problem of the unsightly exposed cistern in this case? The solutions are there and they are various:

✓ You could have a counter wall created to be placed against the existing one made with thin 3 cm tiles. You would then have a total thickness of 11 centimeters (in addition to the plaster) sufficient to place a recessed box
✓ Create a lightweight counterwall (plasterboard) behind the toilet and bidet only where all the pipes and the cistern are to be housed. In this way you avoid touching the wall behind the Drain Cassette in the counterwall.
✓ You could choose a toilet with an external design cistern; now, there are some very beautiful solutions.

Problem 3: the correct distribution of sanitary ware in the bathroom

Now comes the most interesting part: what is the best arrangement of the fixtures in the bathroom? Of course, everyone will tell you: "it depends on the shape of your bathroom, every situation is different". This is not the case. In fact, if it is true that you have to adapt each solution to your specific case, there are small rules dictated by practice and common sense that I advise you to respect in order not to have bad results.

1. What do you need to see first when you enter a bathroom?

When you enter a bathroom the first thing you see must NEVER be the toilet and bidet. It is true that we are talking about a bathroom but it must still be a decent and practical place: when you go to the bathroom you usually use the toilet, wash your hands and then go out. So, the closest thing to the door, or the first thing you see, should be the sink. If you can't find any solution to put the sink near the door then try to put the bathtub or shower there, which are often two beautiful objects to see. (Of course, if this is not possible, there is no law that forbids you to put the toilet in front of the door!)

2. Where do you have to put the toilet?

The ideal location is by the window. The reason I think you can figure it out for yourself: the smells leave the room faster. Also, in case it is not possible, try to put it as close as possible to the window. (In fact, it often happens that, for reasons of space, you are forced to put the shower or bathtub near the window. In this case, put the toilet next to the shower).

3. First the bidet or the toilet?

What I wrote to you in the previous paragraph should already give you an idea of what the ideal arrangement should be: first the bidet and immediately after the toilet.

Always remember one concept: try to put the thing that gives you the strongest dirty feeling, the toilet, as far as possible from the entrance to the bathroom (of course, I'm not telling you that your toilet is dirty!).

4. Where do I put the shower (or tub)?

There is no precise rule. The shower and the bathtub are one of the predominant elements in the bathroom (given the size) so there are two factors:

- ✓ Wherever you put it, it is visible.
- ✓ You never know where to put it (especially if the bathroom is not very big).

The best location would be in front of the bidet / toilet unit. However, this needs a considerable width of bathroom, which is often not possible.

A second solution could be, in a narrow and long bathroom where all the fixtures are located along one wall, insert it between the sink (located near the entrance to the bathroom) and the bidet / toilet unit. With this solution you have to make sure that the space in front of the shower is large enough to pass through easily.

We will explore the dimensions and distances in the next paragraph, but keep in mind that if you position the shower in this way you need at least 60 centimeters to pass easily. A third solution, which is the one that allows greater space optimization in many cases, is to insert the shower where you would never think: under the window. Also, in this case, it

[19]

is an optimal solution for narrow and long bathrooms, in fact you can have a very large shower (as wide as the whole bathroom) and that will not bother you. The only precaution is to replace the window panes with frosted glass.

The two typical examples

Of course, there are many possible variables, and it all really depends on the shape and size of your bathroom, so an ad hoc solution must almost always be studied. But the small rules that I have listed above are valid in all cases and adapt perfectly to the two most common forms of bathrooms that can be found inside condominiums:

- ❖ The narrow and long bathroom
- ❖ The square bathroom

In reality, the first case (narrow and long bathroom) is clearly the most widespread form: almost all condominium apartments have a bathroom with these proportions because, being considered a service space, it is obtained by trying to waste as little space as possible in favor of the other main areas.

The ideal arrangement in the narrow and long bathroom

If you need to renovate a bathroom of this type, the best solution is always to put all the sanitary ware on one wall. The best sequence is: sink, bidet, toilet and shower / tub under the window.

The ideal layout in the square bathroom

If, on the other hand, you have a square bathroom, the situation is a little different: of course, you cannot put all the sanitary ware on one wall but you will probably be forced to distribute them on two opposite walls.

Always remember, if possible, to put the bidet and toilet side by side. If you do not have enough space, place the bidet and toilet opposite each other with the toilet next to the shower and the bidet next to the sink. These are of course all practical tips but remember that in any case, the position of the door and drain command the disposition of the suite components: the closer to the drain the toilet is the fewer problems you will have.

5. The dimensions and the right distances between the sanitary ware

It is important that you know how much the living space around each sanitary is because it is easy, for those who are not experts, to make mistakes by placing the sanitary ware too close to each other and thus making the bathroom difficult to use. These are simple ergonomic measures that will help you define the layout of your new bathroom in detail.

The sink

How big is a sink? There are the standard sizes, i.e. those of the classic ceramic washbasin with the column underneath (about 60 centimeters in width by about 50 centimeters in depth) and then there are the measures of what is now actually installed, i.e. designer sink tops, with the most disparate shapes and sizes. If the bathroom you are renovating is the main one in your home, then the advice is to think of a sink surface that is about 90 centimeters wide and between 50 and 55 centimeters deep: it is certainly more comfortable.

As for the living space that must be on the sides, just think about how you use the sink: you put yourself in front of it. Considering the standard sink it is sufficient to leave 10 centimeters to the left and 10 centimeters to the right of the sink to allow optimal use. If, on the other hand, you want to opt for a more generously sized sink, you can easily ignore the space needed on the sides, indeed you could even lean it against a side wall without problems. Remember, however, if the sink is near the door, to make sure that it can open without bumping into it.

The bidet

The dimensions of almost all models of bidets and toilets are standard: 38 centimeters wide by 55 centimeters deep. From here it is a little different, unless you are looking for small bathroom fixtures for a very small bathroom. For the

space needed on the sides, even in this case, I invite you to think about how you use the bidet: you straddle it. So, when thinking about how to put it in your bathroom you need to keep in mind that you need, on both sides, enough space to put your legs: 25 centimeters is more than enough space (unless you are 2 meters tall!). Keep in mind a detail that can help you save space: if the bidet will often be next to the sink and if the latter will be of the classic type (i.e. the one with the column below and not with a cabinet), the distance between the sink and the bidet it can be reduced to only 10 centimeters, because one leg will end up under the sink. On the other hand, of course, you will still need about 25 centimeters.

The toilet

We have already said about the dimensions when talking about the bidet, for the space instead the reasoning to be done is a little different.

The toilet can be used in two ways: if you are a man, on some occasions you put yourself in front of it (standing), in all other cases (men and women) you have to sit on it. Therefore, the strictly necessary space is that of the toilet itself. But for convenience it is always good to have at least 15 centimeters per side of free space. Clearly if on one side (as it is likely to be) there is the bidet, on that side you will have to have the 25 centimeters we were talking about above.

One thing you have to pay attention to is the space that must be in front of all these components: the minimum living space is about 60 centimeters. Although they may seem few, keep in mind that these are objects that are located below your point of view, so you do not have the impression of being in a very narrow space as if you were in a 60 cm wide corridor. Having said that, the advice is to try to have at least 70-80 cm in front of these sanitary fixtures, to ensure greater comfort. If your bathroom is narrow you can try to look for a smaller toilet and bidet model on the market: there are many and they are absolutely no more uncomfortable than the classic ones.

The shower (or tub)

In the case of a shower, you must always pay attention to a fundamental point: access to the shower must be free of any obstacles: I have found showers whose access was made practically impossible by the presence of a bidet and toilet right in front.

In this case you do not have space problems on the sides, indeed if you can lean it against two contiguous walls it is even better. The important thing is that there are at least 60 centimeters in front of the entrance door to the shower cabin. Keep in mind that a standard shower is 80 × 80 centimeters in size, but it's easy to find smaller or rectangular ones. But always remember: a shower must never have any side smaller than 70 centimeters and in this case, it would be preferable for the second side to be longer, to give more space inside. For the bathtub, the matter is similar to the shower, although perhaps even simpler: make sure you have enough space to get in and that's it. Do you want to know the size of a bathtub? I could answer you: any size you want. In fact, even the standard dimensions of a rectangular tub start from a tiny 120 × 70 cm to reach 200 × 90 cm. The most common in the bathrooms of the apartments is 180cm x 70cm wide. Now you know everything about the bathroom: the problems you may encounter, how to arrange the bathroom fixtures, what size they are, what distances they have to keep. Finally, the time has come to choose the type of bathroom fixture and the floor and wall finishes.

Problem 4: bathroom finishes

This will surely be the shortest paragraph: we have already said that you can find thousands of articles that tell you about finishes for your bathroom and here I would not add anything new, but a couple of tips that nobody tells you I would like to try anyway. give them to you.

Renovation

Non-slip bathroom tiles. If you decide to cover the floor and walls with tiles, remember that the tiles you will place on the ground must be non-slip and impact resistant. In fact, usually the tiles that go to the wall are of a softer paste that splinters easily (of course if something falls on them ... they are just fine on the wall) and being often glazed when they get wet, they become slippery, making you risk a tumble after a shower. Just ask the dealer or company that does the work for you to quickly resolve this possible problem.

If your bathroom is small, or it is narrow and long, I advise you to put large tiles (60cm x 60cm) in order to give the impression that it is larger. Better if rectified, i.e., cut in such a way that they can be laid with an almost imperceptible gap between one tile and another. Clearly, tiles with these characteristics cost significantly more than normal tiles, so don't expect to spend little and have high-quality materials. But keep in mind that the bathroom is usually small, so it is almost always a few hundred dollars of extra material.

Is there only ceramic for the bathroom?

Concrete and resin cladding. The answer is of course no: the idea that the bathroom floor and walls must necessarily be covered with ceramic tiles is wrong. It is true that mostly waterproof materials are needed (especially on the ground if you don't want to flood the downstairs tenant), but there are many other solutions.

I will mention only one that is currently having a good diffusion: resin. It is a material that is good in the bathroom as it is waterproof and therefore does not let water pass through the floor and protects the walls. It can also be obtained in an almost infinite quantity of finishes and being continuous it manages to make your bathroom seem much larger than it actually is.

As I promised you this paragraph was very short. Now let's move on to the next one (the last of this chapter) which I guess is the one that interests you the most.

Problem 5: how much does it cost to renovate the bathroom?

If you remember in the chapter in which I told you about the costs of renovating the house, I deliberately omitted to give you precise information on the cost of carrying out the work.

I invite you to read it if you have not already done so because all the costs that you will have to incur are explained there in addition to those of the work.

The reason why I didn't tell you about the costs of carrying out the works there is that generalizing for a varied territory like Italy is extremely difficult to give valid values for all the regions. In this chapter, however, I want to try to give you some orders of magnitude, limiting myself to the cost of the works only, although you must always keep in mind that the only real parameter to evaluate any renovation is a quote drawn up by one or more companies of your area and based on a precise plan and calculation.

Having made this necessary premise, let's understand what works (and costs) are necessary to renovate your bathroom:

- ❖ Demolitions and disposal
- ❖ Masonry works
- ❖ Waterworks
- ❖ Electrical system
- ❖ Finishes and sanitary ware

Let's see them one by one.

1. Demolition and disposal

The company that will carry out the work will have to clean up everything currently in your bathroom (remember that here we are talking about the renovation of your bathroom, not the make-up), so:

It will remove all the fixtures and fittings

It will completely remove the tiles lining the walls

It will remove the plaster under the tiles

It will remove the floor tiles

It will remove the concrete screed that is between the tiles and the load-bearing floor slab

It will remove all the pipes of the systems that were inside the screed, as well as those that were in the walls

Of course, if you have to move walls you will need to add the demolitions of the existing walls

In addition to being demolished, all this material will have to be transported to landfills and disposed of there.

So, in reality you will have to incur 3 costs:

- ✓ Demolitions
- ✓ Transport
- ✓ Disposal

Of course, the final cost of these operations depends on the amount of material and therefore on the size of your bathroom. I guess you don't want to start doing complicated calculations to see how much each single phase of every single work you are going to demolish will cost you, so I'll give you some broad references to understand how much you will spend. (Basically, I tell you: you can spend from very little to very much)

You only need two data: the floor area and the area of all the walls (to calculate it you just need to multiply the length of the wall by its height). ,

For all the plaster and tile demolitions that you will do on the walls you will have to spend approximately $15 to $18 per square meter.

For all floor and screed demolitions you will have to spend approximately $ 22 to $ 26 per square meter. To remove and dispose of sanitary ware and related taps you will have to spend around $ 10 per piece

If you have to change the shape and size of the bathroom to demolish entire walls you will have to spend between $ 20 and $ 22 per square meter

Do you want to know a way to save something?

If once you have removed the tiles from the walls you see that the underlying plaster is in good condition, you can decide not to remove it but to do what is called "smoothing" to bring the walls back perfectly flat. In this way you save both the costs of demolition and disposal of the plaster and a large part of the costs of new plaster.

However, the best advice is always to redo all the plaster

2. Water system

Once the company has made a clean sweep, the most interesting part comes: your new bathroom has to be built. Where do we start? With the plant.

The water system must first be created, which consists of two parts: the water load (hot and cold) and the water discharge (those that go into the sewer). Let's consider a normal bathroom where there are:

✓ A sink
✓ A bidet
✓ A toilet
✓ A shower / bath

[33]

The plumber will have to put a manifold in the bathroom: essentially inside a recessed box (usually hidden behind the door) he will get the general hot and cold-water pipes and from here the pipes that go to each sanitary appliance will start. In addition to the works strictly necessary to create the system, you will also have to consider the necessary masonry works (creation of the niche and the traces to pass the pipes to the wall). So, the costs you will have to incur will be:

✓ Collector: from 200 $ to 300 $
✓ Loading and unloading lines for each appliance from $ 150 to $ 250 per appliance
✓ Masonry works: from $ 200 to $ 300

On balance, a complete plumbing system for your bathroom will cost you from $ 1,000 up to $ 1,600

3. Electrical system

By completely redesigning the bathroom you will also be forced to redo the electrical system: in fact, the regulations currently in force are very different from the old ones and require specific requirements. Fortunately, an electrical system for the bathroom consists of a few elements:

✓ A ceiling light point
✓ A wall light point above the sink
✓ The switches to turn on the lights

Some power sockets (usually no more than 2 or 3), one of which is of the Schuco type (commonly called "German") which must be positioned next to the sink.

Being a small intervention, the total cost of an electrical system for the bathroom hardly exceeds $ 500, including the costs for creating the traces in the wall.

PS: since the electrical system must be certified, check that the electrician who does it can issue the certifications and above all that it respects all the laws on the distances between electrical terminals (lights, sockets and switches) from the water supply points (taps).

4. Masonry works

After having made the systems, you need to move on to the construction works:

- ✓ The screed in the floor including the creation of any steps
- ✓ The plaster on the walls
- ✓ Any masonry if you have moved any walls

Also, in this case, as for demolitions, you will need the surface of the floor and that of the walls.

The average cost for a floor screed ranges from $ 20 to $ 30 per square meter.

The average cost for plaster ranges from $ 18 to $ 25 per square meter.

The average cost for brick walls ranges from $ 20 to $ 35 per square meter.

5. Finishes and Sanitary

Here you can give vent to your imagination: we have already said that the choice is endless and you can find many articles that can give you ideas on this. Unfortunately, the prices of the finishes are also directly proportional to their quality. Let's see together what these finishes are:

❖ Flooring
❖ Wall cladding
❖ Sanitary and taps
❖ Paintings

Bathroom Mosaic

Here I will try to give you only a broad average reference price, but keep in mind, for example, that if you wanted to cover your bathroom with mosaic-like tiles you could end up, just for the supply, having to spend up to over $100 per square meter. So, keeping our feet on the ground, the items that make up the finishes are composed of two parts:

❖ The cost of purchasing materials
❖ The cost of labor required to lay them

Let's try to quantify these costs.

Floors and wall coverings: installation from $ 30 to $ 35 per square meter, supply of materials from $ 20 to $ 50 per square meter (medium / good quality materials). Keep in mind that wall claddings almost never set up to the ceiling (unless you have special aesthetic needs) but often stop at the height of the door, that is 2.1m. The upper part will be painted.

How to save on coatings

A choice to save money is not to cover all the walls of the bathroom with tiles, but only those in direct contact with water (essentially those on which the sanitary fixtures are fixed). You can simply paint the others, making sure to use a suitable paint, possibly anti-mold. The same applies to sanitary ware: laying more supply. In this case the installation can be more expensive because it also includes the installation of the taps. So: installation from $ 80 to $ 120 per piece, cost of bathroom fixtures from $ 150 to $ 400 per piece, taps from $ 50 to $ 150 per piece. Finally, the painting: in fact, it will be essential to repaint the ceiling and the part of the walls not covered with tiles. The cost here will not be high: between $ 5 per square meter and $ 8 per square meter (of course for standard finishes, if you are looking for special effects the cost goes up to over $ 12 per square meter).

6. Various works

A small paragraph is missing: in fact, there are additional works that could give a final touch to your bathroom. One is certainly a false ceiling with the insertion of recessed spotlights. The cost in this case is between $ 30 and $ 40 per square meter, including spotlights.

IS IT POSSIBLE TO RENEW A BATHROOM BY YOURSELF WITHOUT RESORTING TO WORKERS?

You would like to restore your old bathroom yourself, let's see if it is possible and how much it costs us

Restoring the bathroom, useful tips

Redoing the bathroom is an expensive job and if entrusted to specialists, on average, it costs around 5 thousand dollars for a standard bathroom without too many fine finishes such as whirlpool tubs or particularly well-finished shower cabins.

Removing old coatings, tiles, bathroom fixtures, fixing the water and electrical system is certainly not a job that can be done in a day.

The replacement of tiles and sanitary ware as part of ordinary maintenance does not require special authorizations or permits from the municipality, therefore these are works that can be done economically and alone, it is however advisable to inquire with the competent authorities in order to avoid problems with the neighbors caused by noises or nuisances, such as dust, caused by the various processing stages. Also keep in mind that you will take more time than skilled workers and consider in advance the possibility that arise from contingencies.

Costs for cladding and flooring

The cost of materials, which can vary depending on the quality and the price you are willing to spend, has a relative impact on the total, since the bathroom is usually small in size.

Costs for health care

The same reasoning applies to sanitary ware, which vary from very low prices for economic and imported models up to a cost that can reach $ 500 for prestigious models.

Washbasin and furniture

Wanting to make our bathroom a work of art for the washbasin and furniture can spend up to 1,500 $, otherwise we can find good solutions from around 200 dollars or even less for most models. Much depends on your tastes and your budget.

Disposal of special waste

The disposal of material such as building rubble, old tiles and old appliances is a part of the job that can create problems and difficulties, we need to find a qualified center, usually provided free of charge but usually people are surprised by the quantity produced and your car will certainly not be enough to do all the work.

Redoing a bathroom, yourself has a cost, all in all, affordable, just $1,000 dollars may be enough for the bathroom suite, however, being a job that has many critical issues which could affect the future, such as loss of water or tiles that come off, the help of a professional can be recommended at least for the most delicate operations.

How to redo a do-it-yourself bathroom

We list the main operations to be carried out.

1) Dismantle the old bathroom fixtures / furniture and clear out the bathroom

In order to redo the bathroom, it is necessary to disassemble everything. To disassemble the bathroom fixtures just remove the screws that anchor them to the ground and pull them gently until they detach from the ground, they are usually anchored to the ground by means of screws and white concrete, be careful not to hit them too hard to avoid breaking them and damaging the pipes.

2) Removal of tiles / floors

If you are going to replace old siding and tiles, a mallet and flat-tipped chisel removing the tiles and siding is a pretty quick operation. With the mallet and the chisel just pry the tip between the screed / wall and the edge of the tiles with small strokes. This operation must be done on the floor after having destroyed one, it is a tiring operation but with half a day a single person can easily dismantle the surface of a standard-sized bathroom.

3) Removing the old glue

This operation is definitely the longest and most tiring, under the tiles you will find the old adhesive on top of the concrete screed, to do a good job you have to remove it all by uncovering the screed so that you can reposition the new tiles without raising the top. You have to very patiently chip away at the adhesive in various directions to remove it completely, it may take more than a full day for a large bathroom.

4) Collection and disposal of waste

There is a lot of waste produced by a renovation of the bathroom. It must be collected in special sacks for masonry and disposed of at an authorized center.

5) Laying the tiles

Making a floor is a simple operation but if you have no experience you have to pay close attention, you have to lay the tiles in an order established according to your aesthetic preferences, using adhesive and cutting the tiles with precision.

6) Assembly of the new sanitary ware

At this point it is necessary to do the opposite of disassembly, that is to reposition them in their established place, taking care to properly mount the gaskets, make the holes to anchor the sanitary fixtures to the ground, and screw them down.

In conclusion: The bathroom is not exactly a job suitable for DIY unless you have a second bathroom available, a lot of patience and desire to learn, to make a DIY bathroom it could take us even more than a week and often for those who do not have all this time it is better to resort to professionals or at least to help for the most delicate parts.

Example of a DIY bathroom makeover expense:

- ❖ Bathroom upholstery: 200 dollars
- ❖ New sanitary: 300 dollars
- ❖ Shower plate and shower cabin: 250 dollars
- ❖ New taps: 300 dollars
- ❖ Washbasin with cabinet: 200 dollars
- ❖ Pieces of pipe, fittings, gaskets: 50 dollars
- ❖ 80 l water heater: 90 dollars
- ❖ Help of a Plumber: 200 dollars

Total expense: 1590 dollars

HOW TO FURNISH A SMALL BATHROOM: LITTLE TRICKS

To furnish a small bathroom it takes few, but important elements.

Generally, when you have to furnish a small bathroom, you worry about the speck in the eye and leave out the beam.

The most frequent doubts are:

- ❖ What color do you recommend?
- ❖ How do I arrange the sanitary facilities?
- ❖ Should the shower be installed near the window?
- ❖ Square or rectangular tiles?
- ❖ How about resin?
- ❖ How do I put up the lights?
- ❖ Can I use wallpaper?

Let's dispel a myth immediately.

Not all donuts come with a hole. Not even the bathrooms, in fact, and there are many houses, perhaps more than you can imagine, that have a bathroom maybe too small, or too narrow, or badly planned. You should, therefore, arrange well, during the design phase, the elements that characterize it.

If you are struggling with a renovation, you may want to write down the things that do not work in the old environment and improve them accordingly.

Consider that moving the drains is often not easy and therefore if you want to proceed with an economical renovation, leave the position of the toilet and at least of the shower intact. The distances to be respected are simple, but they must be considered well, in fact making mistakes is very easy, so find yourself with a non-functional bathroom is a moment. There is very small sanitary ware on the market, the dimensions of the toilet and bidet are about 40cm wide and 55cm deep but there are also smaller ones, like 40x50cm.

The toilet must be positioned at least 15-20cm from the next wall. The bidet at least 20cm, between the toilet and the bidet there must be at least 20-25cm. The sink has a depth of about 45-50cm, the small tub is 70x170cm, while the shower minimum is 80x80cm.

All sanitary ware must have a space in front (passage and use) of at least 55cm.

The bidet is not always indispensable, there are toilets with hydrobrush or very effective sanitizing systems that make up for the lack, so the bidet is really a good element to be used only in case of sufficient space.

SHOWER OR BATH?

If the bathroom is very small, it is better to install a shower while a bathtub for showering is not always functional and takes up more space.

Once these basic concepts have been assimilated, it is possible to move on to a more advanced stage of design.

Of course, we are talking about small but memorable bathrooms, not standard bathrooms.

It is always important to put an original touch, so even furnishing a small bathroom is an opportunity, not to be wasted, to do something special.

Returning to the discussion above, after having established the dimensions and distances of the various bathroom fixtures, it is possible to start thinking about colors and coatings.

We start from an assumption. We are talking about a small bathroom, so we do not have large wall surfaces to exploit and fresh air at will.

We basically have two needs:

[47]

❖ Take advantage of all the spaces
❖ Make it look bigger

From which two solutions arise:

Obtain niches or use minimal-looking containment columns. An alternative could be to reuse an old grandmother's sideboard to convert it into a bathroom cabinet with a countertop sink. But only if the size of the whole allows it.

To make a small or very small bathroom seem larger, clear or continuous (resin) coatings must certainly be chosen. The floor could also be decorated light and dark, but the overall mood must be bright.

In general, taking care of the cosmetic aspect of each room is always highly recommended.

An economical but functional trick is to use huge mirrors, even full-wall, that can give a sense of depth by widening the surfaces, but they must be placed as visible as possible from the entrance to the bathroom, otherwise they will not be of any use.

Entering a small bathroom and having the toilet as the first visual element is not the best. Better to see a nice sink, or a walk-in shower.

If, due to various design constraint's it is not always possible to obtain the maximum effect, in many cases something can be done.

Before talking about colors and finishes, I have to say a few words on a very important topic, namely light.

Make the most of natural light, so we make large windows or, if possible, even increase the size, it will be good for the environment, both in terms of aesthetics and hygiene and air quality. In any case, the windows, albeit small, must be enhanced.

NO to curtains if the bathroom is already dark, or use soft curtains completely on one side to enhance the verticality. Let's say for furnishing use only.

Moving on to artificial lighting, to furnish a small bathroom you need general light (spotlights or suspension or ceiling light or LED strip), one in the shower and one directed on the sink for the make-up / shaving area.

When the environment allows it, you can create a full-height LED effect that enhances its depth.

Clearly you will lose a few centimeters if you decide to do it on the wall (on the ceiling it is more convenient when the bathroom is very, very small), but the general mood will be one of a kind.

In order not to make a mistake or not to increase the visual chaos, in these cases propose to create a homogeneous coating, at least in color.

You have to decide whether to give priority to the lighting effect or to the decoration. I see the coexistence of both in a narrow environment difficult.

Coverings for a small bathroom

Approaching the design of a bathroom, we have to decode the style I want to give it: witty, therefore young, elegant, minimalist, dark.

This choice already affects a whole series of materials and finishes that are the direct consequence of it.

In general, for a young mood (perhaps for a single person or a young couple), it can be done with a few touches of color on the small stoneware tiles. For a stately home, better the elegance of materials with stone or earth tones.

The same approach can also be used for historic houses or houses with wooden ceilings.

Minimalism is always recommended, but the fact remains that the unique character of the bathroom should always come out. In this case, to the minimalism of the materials (for example total white or resin or micro-cement) some luminous effect or a precious suspension.

The dark bathroom, more masculine or in any case suitable for very contemporary or industrial contexts, where there is at least another dark approach to the rest of the house.

What is definitely to be avoided are classic bathrooms in modern contexts.

How to cover the walls

Let's say that in general you do not have the obligation to cover all the walls. Rather. You would be wrong to do so.

Those not subject to splashes or wear can be left free, to hang pictures or containing columns, yes pictures look good even in the bathroom.

In theory, you can do as you please on the heights of the coatings, just use an enamel paint to always be calm.

Of course, you should always cover the shower with tiles, large stoneware slabs or suitable wallpaper.

Even if the materials you have installed have a tsunami-proof seal and durability, there will always be new pieces or novelties on the market that will make you think in a decade or so that you've got it all wrong, that the shower door would have been better in a single crystal without edges, that the drop mixer is cooler, that the suspended sanitary fixtures are more comfortable, that the shower tray is no longer used.

So, don't worry now about what it will be in 10 or 15 years.

A house is a living environment, which is transformed and must be accompanied in this process.

Organize your furniture in a small bathroom

An important thing is the general organization of the space, ok with niches, shelves, towel racks and shelves, the important thing is that there is order both in how the various objects are arranged and in the colors.

Maybe you have created a stone effect bathroom, with a beautiful light and all white, suspended and minimalist sanitary ware, then on the top of the sink you go to place toothbrushes, hair dryers, perfumes, jewels and creams, towels and soaps taken from everywhere.

The overall effect will be one of visual chaos, so all the preliminary work will be for nothing.

If you have multicolored creams and soaps, before trashing them, think about placing them in clutches or containers that are not visible.

Place the toothbrushes in a tall toothbrush holder, in order to hide the handles, or buy them all white.

Ditto for the towels.

Obviously, the visual chaos concerns not only the accessories, but also the coverings. Try to minimize joints by using large slabs or rectified tiles or continuous coatings. Let's say that a mosaic effect is not so practical both for the chaos it generates and because the thousand joints tend to blacken and are difficult to clean.

During the renovation, creating an anteroom with a built-in cupboard that contains a washing machine, a stacked dryer and an airing cupboard is an excellent solution. This is a little trick to not ruin the design of the bathroom and to also leave out the noises and dust of washing or drying clothes, which would prevent relaxation. If it is not possible to obtain a dressing room, then ok to the washing machine, but always hidden.

In a service toilet it can also be visible, but let's say that this solution does not inspire me.

THE CORRECT METHOD VS THE PRACTICAL METHOD

The complexity of a bathroom

Before leaving, I must make a premise: in the renovation of a bathroom the factors (people, materials, techniques) that come into play are numerous and must be thought out, coordinated, fitted together and managed with skill.

To do it in the right way you need aesthetic and stylistic knowledge, space management skills, attention to ergonomics, organization of the various elements inside the bathroom, plant and technological knowledge, ability to

[54]

manage implementation times ... In short, you might think that paying so much attention to a single room is excessive ... but I must warn you: renovating the bathroom is not a joke!

Renovating the bathroom, from before to after

The bathroom designer

The first step, which avoids a lot of problems, is the correct design of the environment that you should entrust to a qualified and experienced professional. He will have the role of anticipating problems, thinking about chronological joints, coordinating the elements in a harmonious way.

The construction manager for the renovation

If, then, the same person is instructed to perform the execution of the works, he will have to organize a program in which each operator performs a specific action at a predetermined time, possibly without hitches, errors or delays. And if there are problems (the renovation of a bathroom almost always presents surprises) he will have to act promptly. The renovation of a bathroom must be coordinated in order to have a satisfactory final result in a short time.

Redoing the bathroom, useful tips!

These listed are just a few mistakes to avoid, further useful tips are:

1. The choice of bathroom fixtures

If you're lucky, and you can afford to choose both a suspended and a floor model, consider these tips:

Do you have a wooden floor? If you want to avoid damaging the floor during cleaning, choose suspended sanitary ware

Do you like the minimalist style? Don't make the mistake of choosing bathroom fixtures detached from the wall. The flush-to-the-wall sanitary ware hides all the connections and technical fittings

Is the wall on which you will install the sanitary ware only 8 cm thick? Consider that building a wall in adherence to be able to install the suspended ones would take up space. If your bathroom is narrow, avoid the counter-wall and choose floor-mounted sanitary ware instead, there are some with beautiful designs.

Are you very tall and for convenience would you like sanitary fixtures higher from the floor?

Choose the suspended model. The plumber, if notified in advance, will be able to adjust the fixings to give you the comfort you are looking for

2. Better a bath or a shower?

If you have only one bathroom, you will find yourself having to make a decision: "better a comfortable and relaxing bathtub or a more practical shower?" If you are lucky and have more than one bathroom, you will wonder if at least one should have a bathtub, because you never know ... It can always be useful to have it to dedicate a little time to yourself or perhaps to make it easier for children to bathe!

The tub

Whatever your reason for asking this question, remember that you are not the only one in this situation. The tub has not gone into disuse, quite the contrary! It has returned with a whole new strength.

The shower

But even the shower nowadays has a whole new use. Obviously, it is also dedicated to personal cleanliness, but this, which was once the main reason for "taking a shower", has now become a marginal reason.

The showers can be customized, studied and designed in a tailor-made way in order to be for those who will also use them a wellness tool, in short, a way to be able to take care of themselves and their body without resorting to the tub!

3. Faucets: better built-in or external? And in what material?

Here's another nice dilemma ...

We often let ourselves be guided by the installer who obviously recommends the easiest choice, that is external taps but if we look at magazines and catalogs the trend of the moment is to propose built-in taps.

Built-in or external shower taps?

It means less masonry, fewer traces, ease of replacing parts or the entire set in the future, but also less comfort and it becomes almost impossible to customize.

I am referring above all to the shower taps. The showers I design are usually very large (this is the request made to me by almost all customers in the shop: to have a shower as large as possible!) And to have generous shower spaces you need to think of a built-in tap to make the most of this space!

Mixers in the bathroom: brass or steel?

There is not only chromed brass for taps!!! Fortunately, today we can make a more informed choice, which protects the health of those who will use the water at home and also the environment... Welcome (or rather welcome back) steel!

REDOING A BATHROOM? USEFUL IDEAS AND TIPS TO NOT BE DISAPPOINTED

Before thinking about how much it costs to renovate a bathroom, it is good to consider that this environment is one of the most used in the whole house, as well as being one of the most delicate to get your hands on.

Pipes, electrical systems, gasket sealing and space management: the pitfalls are around the corner and, before going to the savings, it is good to remember that a mistake during the renovation could be very expensive, other than modest prices and all inclusive.

The bathroom makeover is a classic of home renovation, whether we are talking about small renovations or a structural rebuild.

The reasons for doing this can be many: the sink that you no longer like or the family that has grown, the accidental breakage of the shower tray or even a leak from the ceiling; there are a thousand and one reasons for arranging, renovating or recreating a bathroom, starting the process of economic evaluation on labor costs and prices of accessories.

The types of intervention on a bathroom to be restored

Let's start from the basics: there are different degrees of intervention to which a bathroom can be subjected when we talk about renovations. Let's see the main ones, trying to understand their characteristics also in terms of expenditure.

Moving or creating from scratch - We are facing the most complex and expensive case, that is to create a bathroom from scratch or move the previous one to a different location in the home. To obtain the desired result, you must necessarily touch other areas of the house, increasing costs.

Total renovation - That is when the renovation involves: demolition of portions of masonry, laying of tiles, moving of plumbing and electrical systems, replacement of sanitary ware.

Put simply, completely redoing a pre-existing bathroom.

Partial renovation - A minor intervention, without masonry work, which involves only coatings, sanitary ware and related systems.

We are facing the recurring type of work of those who want to redo a bathroom and expect not to spend an excessive amount, relying on false beliefs such as: "so much are they just a sink and a shower" and "a friend of mine did it with a few dollars"; better to do the math well, because the factors that can drive up prices, as we will see, are many.

Renovation and relook - less invasive intervention that should make you spend less working only on painting, choice of furnishings, replacement of sanitary ware without plumbing and improvements to lighting. In fact, the tiling remains outside, which would make the intervention fall into the previous category; in place of the tiler's job, however, it is possible to include the laying of low-thickness ceramics and vinyl materials directly on existing tiles and floors in the redoing of a bathroom.

This clear division is useful to have as a yardstick when talking to a professional, but we will never find these terms in an official proposal because the total cost of renovating a bathroom depends on too many factors to be simplified in this way.

What affects the cost of renovating a bathroom? Let's make a list.

Square footage

It might seem strange and not very logical, but the difference in square meters does not affect the cost to be considered to redo a bathroom. Of course, we will need more tiles and more paint for the walls when dealing with larger rooms, but the bulk of the shopping will come from other elements such as systems or furnishings, as we will see in the next points.

Installations

The bulk of the expense in the renovation of the bathroom is decided by the renovation works. In fact, putting your hand to pipes and manifolds means going to work on floors and walls, in case of problems with the general plumbing of the apartment, even outside the bathroom.

There are two systems to consider: the loading one carries and distributes the water to the sanitary fixtures, the drain one takes care of draining the black water. The technical characteristics of the system - with single or double pipes, in PVC or steel, with one or more collectors - do not count for much in terms of expenditure, the problem is how much of the entire network of pipes and connections will have to be redone.

Take for example a new apartment with manifolds, pipes, distribution columns and drainage wells in the right position: in this case the intervention will only concern the connection of the sanitary ware and the testing. A different case than that of an old independent house where it was decided to move the bathroom; here the whole system will have to be put back into operation by working on walls, floors and, in the worst case, also on the main pipes that carry water from the building's water network.

Needless to say, how much the presence or absence of masonry works affects the cost of a plumbing system which, as we have seen, can transform a simple partial refurbishment into a real construction site, consequently increasing costs.

Materials

The objects that you can install in a bathroom are more or less always the same: sink, cabinet, tub / shower, bathroom fixtures, lights, tiles, accessories and little else. Yet, for each one, the cost can drastically change even just for the material used, economic or valuable:

- ❖ chipboard / solid wood
- ❖ laminate / stone
- ❖ industrial terracotta / porcelain
- ❖ plastic / crystal

You pay for quality, and this applies to the choice of materials as well as to those who make the supplies, as we will see in the following point.

Furnishings

We talked about redoing a large or small bathroom, completely or partially, with materials of different qualities; now all that remains is to face an expense item that can greatly increase costs: the choice of the manufacturer of accessories, bathroom fixtures and furnishings.

On the one hand, we can choose the quality, design and reliability of internationally known Italian and foreign manufacturers, brands whose models appear in printed and online magazines as examples of the best bathroom furniture. On the other hand, we have the same types of furnishings and accessories, only in the large DIY store version.

The economic difference between the two alternatives can vary a lot, and not only for the quality of the materials, which we have already talked about, but also for the accuracy in the construction and the research of the design.

Regardless of the quality, the function of the furniture and accessories remains unchanged - you can brush your teeth, take a shower and everything else - but the yield changes over time as well as the personal appeal.

A good product will tend to remain in good condition over the years and will be a pleasure to see every day, perfectly integrated into the overall look of your bathroom. You will then have a wide variety of choices between the different manufacturers, something that is lacking with mass production, which tends to standardize variants, models and sizes to reduce costs.

Living costs: or what we find on the invoice

When we talk about the renovation of a bathroom, the same precautions apply as for any professional work on a property, including the calculation of all those items that are often associated with the pure renovation work: the so-called living costs.

- ❖ Opening and making the site safe
- ❖ Demolition and disposal of waste materials
- ❖ Building practices - only in the case of moving walls
- ❖ Repairs and finishes at the end of the works
- ❖ Various transport and raising to the floor
- ❖ Final survey and document drafting

These are just some examples of the items that you could find on the invoice, where a lot also depends on the type of requests made and the extent of the interventions. All these items must be included in the proposal specifications that the executing company provides before the actual invoice, so that everything can be reviewed point by point.

It is also advisable, in the case of works that have taken over during construction, to put everything in writing (also by email), so as not to incur misunderstandings when closing the works.

When it comes to the cost of renovating a bathroom, we therefore stay away (or at least pay attention) to all those ads, online and otherwise, where fixed prices are proposed without specifying anything.

To get started on the right foot, get an idea of the work to be done, take some measurements (which can always be useful) and contact two or more professionals for an inspection with the most detailed estimate possible - please, all free.

Okay, but in the end how much do you spend to redo the bathroom?

Better get over it: there is no price list for the renovation of the interior of a building, much less a bathroom. Those who propose it to you do so on the basis of experience, as well as interest, but rather than real costs we are dealing with expense indications calculated in square meters and on the average of the works already carried out.

The only rule we would like to give you is that of common sense, seasoned with a little attention: to renovate a bathroom you spend as much as you can, for what you need, for how much effort you want to put in and on the basis of the risks that you are willing to take in the event that you have to put your hand back on a restructuring work done badly by others or with friends or acquaintances.

BATHROOM CLADDING HEIGHT: HINTS AND IDEAS

How has the bathroom coating trend changed in recent times?

The covering of the walls and floor of the bathroom is one of the first things to choose when starting to furnish this room of the house: a choice that has undergone several changes over time both with respect to the aesthetics of the surface and the laying methods.

In the past, the laying height of the tile varied from 1.2 to 1.5 meters from the ground up to the middle of the wall, leaving the upper section uncovered, which remained white; a practice that is still quite consolidated in some Italian regions and also abroad, where other materials are often used to cover, in addition to ceramics.

An alternative to this solution today consists in creating the covering up to the height of the door, that is from 2 to 2.2 meters, thus allowing to be less constrained on the design of the tile, choosing to insert different colors or surface divisions to obtain dynamic and unique patterns. The uncovered part is therefore only in the conjunction with the ceiling, to be refreshed from time to time.

In recent years, bathroom walls have enjoyed a solution more modern and practical, set the tiles to the ceiling. The result is pleasant and elegant: the vertical parts are made compact, the linearity is enhanced, the joints are almost invisible, thanks to the installation of large format tiles. Excluding the ceiling, there is no longer the need for periodic whitewashing and the walls are easy to clean and completely protected from mold and humidity. Moreover, innovation of materials has permitted the realization of antibacterial sheets, such as ceramic surfaces able to eliminate up to 99.9% of bacteria.

The aesthetics of the surface is rather geared towards a choice of colors; the preference of neutral tones, very popular because they promote relaxation and intimacy in the bathroom, or decorative solutions give character and personality to the space. Full-wall coverings, in the name of functionality and aesthetic refinement, represent the latest trend for bathroom coverings, available in different styles, colors and surfaces to meet every need.

HOW TO DECORATE THE BATHROOM CEILING

Would you like to give a touch of personality to your home but don't know how to decorate the bathroom ceiling? Here are some original ideas and some tips for decorating the bathroom ceiling, transforming a flat room into an environment of character and style all its own. If your trusted architect has advised you to renovate the bathroom for a fortune, but your budget is very little or almost nothing, you just have to sharpen your wits and find some alternative solution. Expensive and precious coatings for your walls and ceiling can have a great impact on the room, but they will have an equally disruptive impact on your finances: the time has come to make the most of furnishing elements such as plays of lights, frames, decorations and plasterboard and give vent to all our creativity.

Stencil for the bathroom ceiling

A perfect solution for decorating the ceiling of your bathrooms are certainly stencils: a ductile and easy-to-apply solution, stencils can be used not only to decorate your ceiling but also the floor, creating an element of continuity within the environment.

Many decorations are available, decorations that will satisfy all tastes: abstract motifs, classic motifs, leaves, flowers and plants in stencil version have a low cost and will allow your bathroom to be transformed with a minimum investment and easy application. If, on the other hand, your home embodies

[69]

the antique or classic style, you could consider the opportunity to fall back on drawings and frescoes to decorate both the walls and the ceiling (perhaps in perfect Art Nouveau style, an always elegant style).

Decorate the bathroom ceiling with paint

If stencils and frescoes aren't your thing, you could always consider the simplest solution: color. Taking advantage of a colored paint that matches the context, you could use a natural sponge to create a soft gradient effect. Before moving on to using the sponge, however, we advise you to paint the surface with a neutral color in order to create a uniform base on which to create the shades.

Panels for the ceiling

This solution is ideal for those modern and design bathrooms that make the most of geometric shapes and strong lines: we are talking about decorative panels, a fairly economical solution not recommended only in the case of a sloping roof house.

In this case, therefore with sloping roof houses, it is generally preferable to use fake beams to maintain the rustic style: the beams, once installed, can be painted (with colors matched to the bathroom) or left in the natural color (wood).

False ceiling and light effects to decorate the bathroom

Plasterboard is certainly one of the most used solutions in recent years: not only does it allow us to model the bathroom according to our needs, but it offers infinite possibilities for decorating the ceiling: in addition to creating new volumes and new spaces, plasterboard offers the opportunity to create unique plays of light, using spotlights and directional lights to create depth and design effects.

HOW TO REMOVE MOLD IN THE BATHROOM

Mold in the bathroom is so widespread that some people think it's normal.

Who said it is normal to have mold in their bathroom?

If you think about it, the bathroom is the place where we are often naked, therefore more defenseless towards molds, and we know it is not good for health.

Why you have to think that it is normal to have black mold on your head while brushing your teeth or taking a shower is not very clear.

We use the toothbrush and the antibacterial toothpaste and the natural PH shower gel and then ...

What causes mold in the bathroom?

To form mold, water is needed to "water" the invisible mold spores that settle on walls and objects, so eliminating all mold spores from homes would be an impossible task, but it is possible not to feed the spores and so don't have them turn into mold.

The most frequent way for which water forms on the walls that gives life to molds is in the form of condensation.

There may be leaks or broken pipes but condensation moisture is the main cause.

Contrary to what many thinks, condensation humidity is humidity that is produced in the house by its inhabitants.

Sleeping, a human body emits three glasses of water overnight and laundry hanging produces 3-5 kg. When the hot and humid air meets a sufficiently cold surface the vapor content is condensed, as in the summer when you open the fridge and the bottle or can gets wet with droplets.

[73]

So when you see condensation or mold in the bathroom or in the bedroom you think "there is a lot of humidity", but that's not quite the case, it would be like saying that there is humidity in the fridge or in the can, there is only a colder point, moisture was in the air or it may have formed from normal daily activity.

But if the ambient humidity is excessive, too low temperatures are not needed to have condensation, the coldest points are usually at the top, in the corners in contact with the slab or a beam and the warm and humid air in the bathroom, of course, it forms more than in other rooms, for example after a hot shower and when it comes into contact with a fairly cold wall, it condenses.

THINGS NOT TO DO IF YOU DON'T WANT MOLD IN THE BATHROOM

Some situations increase or favor the formation of condensation and therefore the formation of mold in the bathroom. Let's see them.

1) Use washable paint
2) Walls finished with plasterboard
3) Paints containing organic substances (such as glitter and fancy things or with high VOC)
4) Shower or steam hitting the wall
5) Wall too cold

HABITS AND BEHAVIORS THAT FAVOR MOLD IN THE BATHROOM:

✓ Not heating the bathroom.
✓ With a cold bath, run the hot shower for a long time to "warm up the air"
✓ Not ventilating, especially if a lot of steam has been produced.
✓ Leaving the house dark and cold and the bathroom full of steam.
✓ Leaving the house cold all day, turn up the heating or turn on the stove at high temperature when you return. (Thermal shock)

Why do the above points favor or cause mold to grow in the bathroom?

Washable paint should never be used in the bathroom or in potentially humid rooms, even if it says breathable anti-mold. Washable paint cannot be breathable.

You should devote the same care to finding the correct paint for the bathroom as for the other rooms, while many people instead have a color chosen "at random" for the bathroom.

Non-breathable paints create a surface on which droplets of condensation form more easily.

The paint in the bathroom needs to be refreshed often. It is subjected to the attack of humidity and to a greater deposit of organic substances on the surface of the wall / paint.

Organic substances, skin, poop, fecal bacteria etc. produced in the bathroom, they deposit on the walls and form an invisible "film" which molds love.

Their food is the smallest microorganisms such as bacteria and cellulose (that's why we say drywall is prohibited!)

Plaster walls retain moisture and are not breathable. This favors condensation and the persistence of humidity on the wall. Paints containing volatile organic compounds (VOCs) are not only not very ecological but as you will have understood by now, they are food for molds.

Shower or steam hitting the wall is not good. Use tiles or waterproof materials or change the direction of the jet.

On not heating the bathroom: the colder the bathroom, the colder the air, the walls and top corners will be. Opening the hot water creates steam and by not aerating the humidity it will condense in those colder points.

Using the shower as "heating" also means creating a lot of steam which if not eliminated will condense on the wall. It is fortunate that the mirror will condense a bit and not the wall.

THE WORST HABIT THAT CAUSES MOLD IN THE BATHROOM (OR IN THE HOUSE)

One of the worst habits that cause mold is to leave the house cold for many hours or days and then turn on "full throttle" when you return, this creates a thermal shock.

If you have punctual heating like the legendary pellet stove in the living room, the thing is even more serious, because very hot areas are created and others colder where humidity condenses.

Pellet or wood stoves should go to a dedicated boiler room, never in the living room. One of these cooler areas is obviously the bathroom which always has the door closed.

Another habit is not to use the extractor hood when cooking or to have one that does not expel outside.

The third top habit in the production of humidity and mold is obviously hanging the clothes and ironing without airing or without using a dehumidifier.

Other causes of mold that nobody talks about.

- One thing rarely talked about in relation to molds is cleanliness. Hygiene.
- Leaving dirt in the house or food on the table when you leave.
- Damp or wet clothes that stay for days in the basket in the bathroom or around.
- Sports bag with wet clothes or dirty mud around etc.
- Damp, wet or muddy shoes indoors.
- Animals and humans who bring dirt into the house.

These things introduce a large amount of mold spores, bacteria and moisture.

The other reason is the number of people living in the house.

We happened to do an inspection to find out the cause of the mold and we found 8 people who lived in a small apartment.

Obviously, there was excess moisture and bacteria, even mold on the shelves.

But there is no need to get to these excesses, you just need to host 3 relatives for a week in the winter for the holidays and mold can explode in the house within a day, the more people there are and the more you have to keep clean and ventilate and with modern fixtures there is no air exchange and humidity accumulates, so if you are unable to ventilate the house, controlled mechanical ventilation is required.

Are you starting to think that it is not "natural" to have mold in the bathroom?

Or that you could have a more hygienic bathroom, without that horrible mold that looks at you when you shower? You are right, there is no valid reason to have mold in the bathroom, quite the opposite.

THINGS TO DO TO NOT HAVE MOLD IN THE BATHROOM

They are more or less the opposite of those not to do, let's see them.

Use breathable paints, possibly high-quality anti-mold water-based paint.

Natural lime putty, silicate paint or earthenware which is impermeable to water and can replace tiles. The bathroom should have a non-gypsum settling finish.

Make sure that there are no infiltrations and leaks and that the shower jet does not splash onto the wall, if it is impossible to change it, use a waterproof coating such as tiles, but do not use plasterboard, if you have a false ceiling, cover or divide with slabs using water resistant fiber cement sheets.

Correct behaviors to avoid mold in the bathroom and at home.

1) Keep the bathroom warm. If you can't, turn on a bathroom heater a few minutes before taking a shower.
2) Always ventilate when you shower or create steam in the bathroom.

NOTE: Ventilating does not mean leaving the window open for half an hour or the overhead door for the whole day. This cools the wall even more.

To ventilate means to open well only for a few minutes then close again.

Repeat this several times a day.

3) Do not create thermal shocks in the house. Try to create an average temperature during the day and between the rooms, even if the house remains empty it must not remain frozen or with open windows.

4) When you create more humidity in the kitchen etc., always ventilate, the bedrooms and bathroom are colder than the living areas. Moisture condenses right there and mold forms.

5) Install an extractor in the bathroom. Especially if you have little time to ventilate it is vital to avoid mold in the bathroom, an extractor may also be necessary in the living rooms, there are extractors with humidity sensors that start themselves as soon as the humidity becomes dangerous.

What if mold still forms in the bathroom after all these tips?

If you have a serious mold infestation in your home or if it continually reforms you need professional mold pest control and you need to find out the cause, it could be an infiltration or more likely a serious thermal bridge. Or lack of ventilation. To find out you have to use tools that not everyone has.

Thermal bridge means that you have a corner or a wall that is less insulated or not insulated enough and that acts as a "bridge" with the outside. So, it will "pull in" cold.

The thermal bridge alone is not enough for mold to form, sometimes there are thermal bridges and mold does not form for years, then it arrives and never goes away.

Whatever the cause of the mold, the solution exists.

If you have a serious infestation the first thing to do is a complete disinfestation, which is not done with a sponge and bleach or the supermarket spray, then you have to find the cause so that it does not reform, DIY is often dangerous. And it gets worse, many people trying to clean mold with bleach infest their entire home.

MOLD ON THE BATHROOM CEILING AND NATURAL SOLUTIONS

If mold stains have appeared on the bathroom walls, remember to ventilate more often and solve the problem by choosing one of these natural measures.

The bathroom, as we know, is an environment that easily suffers damage due to humidity, especially if it is not adequately ventilated. It is always helpful, therefore, to know what to do when those ugly mold stains appear on the bathroom ceiling.

The techniques are different, but as you will have understood, the first step is to ensure proper ventilation. Sometimes, however, it is not easy, since the bathroom does not always have large windows like the rest of the house.

Another elementary tip is to make sure that there is no water infiltration in the wall. In this case, the mold stains on the bathroom ceiling could appear within a few days.

Finally, to prevent the formation of mold on the walls, the installation of a good thermal insulator, optimal lighting - preferably natural - and evaluating the arrangement of a dehumidifier or a humidity extractor are ideal.

5 WAYS TO GET RID OF MOLD FROM THE BATHROOM CEILING

Sometimes, no matter how much precautions are taken, mold appears in the corners of the bathroom ceiling. In addition to being aesthetically ugly, mold is above all dangerous to health. For this reason, it is advisable to intervene immediately. Here are some quick and easy anti-mold tips.

1. Borax based cleaning solution

With just a few ingredients it is possible to create a very effective anti-mold solution.

Ingredients

- 2 tablespoons of borax (30 g)
- ¼ cup of vinegar (60 ml)
- 2 cups of hot water (500 ml)

How to proceed?

Mix the ingredients in a spray bottle. Spray the solution on the mold stains. Be sure to cover them and avoid coming into contact with the liquid.

Use gloves and a mask to protect the respiratory tract.

Remove the mold with the abrasive part of a sponge, rinsing it frequently. Once done, spray the solution back onto the stain.

Finally, ventilate the room well and wait for the wall to dry.

At this point it will be necessary to think about the most suitable solution to prevent the formation of new mold on the ceiling or to evaluate a coat of white.

2. Use vinegar

Another good way to get rid of mold on the bathroom ceiling is to use vinegar, a faithful ally in cleaning. Use white vinegar diluted in water.

How to proceed?

Again, you will need to get a bottle with a nebulizer to better reach the mold spot. In very dark spots, where the mold is densest, apply pure vinegar directly.

Even if it is only vinegar, take the precautions already indicated, especially paying attention to the eyes. Also remember that vinegar must never be mixed with bleach as it generates a highly toxic gas.

3. Tea tree oil

It is one of the most powerful natural disinfectants in existence. By preparing a simple solution with this ingredient, you can quickly get rid of mold.

Ingredients

- 2 tablespoons of tea tree oil (30 ml)
- 2 cups of water (500 ml)

How to proceed?

Hand spray mildew cleaner on the bathroom ceiling

With the help of a nebulizer and, of course, wearing gloves, spray this solution on the stains.

In a few minutes they will begin to lighten; after rinsing, the wall will be ready for a good painting; first make sure that the humidity is not caused by water infiltration.

4. Hydrogen peroxide

Although it may be a little less effective than previous solutions, hydrogen peroxide also has an important antibacterial action to offer. It is an ideal solution for small stains or when mold starts to appear on the walls.

How to proceed?

Sprinkle hydrogen peroxide on the stain or apply it with a sponge and let it act. After a quarter of an hour, remove the residues with the help of a brush. If necessary, repeat the process all over again.

Cleaning the tiles: an important step in prevention

Thorough cleaning of the tiles helps to significantly reduce the formation of mold. In addition to ensuring perfect drying of the tiles located around the shower area, it is important to provide for a periodic detailed cleaning of corners and interstices, both of the wall tiles and of the floor tiles. To perform this operation, it will be sufficient to obtain a simple toothbrush (perfect for the cracks between the tiles) and a detergent product that is not too aggressive. Bicarbonate or the detergent that we normally use for dishes, dissolved in water, is also perfect. If we are planning a bathroom makeover, it would be advisable to place tiles on the floor and wall without joints.

Preventing moisture in the bathroom: dehumidifiers and plants

To try to limit condensation in the bathroom, with the consequent formation of mold, some natural measures may be useful. It may be a good idea to place some plants in the bathroom that are known for their ability to improve air quality. These are generally tropical plants, which you can find for sale from a well-stocked nursery. The presence of dehumidifiers applied to the radiators in the room can also help to decrease excess humidity. For an even higher effect it is possible to insert coarse salt inside, keeping it suspended in the tray with the help of a perforated container. The salt will absorb excess water and then deposit it in the dehumidifier tray. Quicklime also manages to give the same results as coarse salt, but requires greater attention in its use. When the salt is excessively wet (generally a period of time of 3/4 days) it will be sufficient to pass it in the oven at a temperature of 50 ° for a quarter of an hour, to then be able to use it again.

Mold is a respectable enemy, but not invincible. Just face it with the right weapons. Adopt one of these tips and don't forget the importance of prevention.

HOW TO CHOOSE A BATHROOM FLOOR

It is possible to lay parquet, pvc, laminate, tile or cork flooring in the bathroom, provided that the floor bears the wording "specially for bathroom". Bathroom floors must necessarily withstand humidity. Maintenance and installation are related to the type.

Technical characteristics of bathroom floors

Each room in the house has its own technical specificities to consider when choosing the floor. The bathroom does not escape the rule, it is not defined as a "frequent passage" room, but it is a wet room. It will therefore be necessary that the choice of the floor of a bathroom is oriented to this characteristic.

In fact, every type of floor is compatible with use in the bathroom, but you need to know its limits (installation, maintenance, resistance, etc.) and choose the suitable variant.

The two main aspects considered in the classification of the use of floors are resistance to abrasion (passage) and resistance to impact.

The bathroom, although obviously used every day, is not a very busy room, unlike the living room for example. You will rarely walk on it in heels, and therefore you will not risk scratching the floor.

The bathroom floor must therefore guarantee a good level of use for a long duration, but there is no need to orient yourself on floors suitable for heavy traffic, more expensive and unnecessary in a bathroom. Choose a floor with a rating of at least 23/31 (high domestic use / light commercial use).

You will have to focus on moisture resistance when choosing your bathroom floor, in a room like the bathroom the floor must have good resistance to humidity, and also a perfect seal, because the bathroom floor is subject to continuous splashes of water and is regularly cleaned. But that is not all! The humidity of the air is very variable within this room and this can affect the floor. In fact, condensation can contribute to moisture stagnation, which is not ideal if the floor is not intended for this use.

Always focus on a certified "bathroom compatible" floor. For all available products, the choice of this type of flooring will inevitably be reduced, but you can always count on the manufacturer's guarantee.

In addition, the floor is a central element in the whole decoration of the room and the bathroom, although small in size, is an important room in the house and you should feel good inside. Whatever type of floor you will be choosing, the choice is wide and floor manufacturers have understood the importance of developing specific products for the bathroom.

Tiles imitate wood, stone or concrete, as do PVC or laminate floors. Any color, look and texture is possible and there is something for everyone, from classic to modern. However, be careful to match floors and wall coverings well. The bathroom is generally a small space. For the floor, avoid large formats that tend to restrict the environment.

It is quite surprising, but any floor can be laid in the bathroom it is enough to comply with the manufacturer's installation and maintenance recommendations. Finally, you will be the one to adapt to the floor!

Tiles: a must in the bathroom

It is the most common type of flooring in the bathroom, in fact, tiles are particularly suitable as they are totally waterproof and easy to maintain. Water cannot penetrate and deform them and this is therefore a great advantage and the tiles can also be installed inside floor-level showers.

There are various models and all your decorative needs can be satisfied: plain or colored, wood, stone, concrete, marble, grit tiles, cement tiles, etc. everything is possible with tiles! An additional, undeniable advantage: tiles can also be installed on the walls in most cases!

Maintenance is very simple thanks to a rag and a cleaning product diluted in water.

The only drawback of the tiles remains the installation, which is rather demanding and binding. Contact a professional if you are unsure, as poorly laid tiles deteriorate very quickly, especially in the bathroom.

PVC and vinyl flooring - an economical choice for the bathroom

PVC and vinyl floors are economical and compatible with the bathroom as they are perfectly waterproof. You can therefore easily opt for this type of flooring in the bathroom. The choice is very wide and you will easily find a floor that suits your tastes. Maintenance is extremely simple, simply vacuum and mop with a neutral cleaning product diluted in water.

The installation is relatively simple for an expert do-it-yourself, both for products in rolls and in sheets (glued or floating installation according to the support and the formats).

Parquet for the bathroom: the choice is crucial

Parquet floors, that is noble wood floors, are not the most suitable for installation in damp rooms such as the bathroom but they are not completely excluded either, the main problem is obviously humidity. Wood is a real sponge and water swells it. The floor could therefore warp quickly if you don't take certain precautions. Avoid pre-finished parquet with floating installation in the bathroom, but go for a glued solid wood, which will resist better and in the same way choose an exotic wood essence such as teak or wenge, more resistant to humidity, make sure that the bathroom is well ventilated so that parquet does not suffer the effects of humidity in the air and as regards the decorative aspect, think of parquet laid in a ship deck to give an original touch to your bathroom.

For maintenance, bathroom parquet floors must often be oiled. Never leave standing water on the wood and periodically oil the parquet (with a microfiber cloth and spray maintenance oil) to preserve its original appearance.

Laminate flooring: the alternative to parquet

Laminate flooring, even if it has a wooden base, is much more stable than parquet. Be careful though, because not all of them are compatible with the bathroom.

Choose well a suitable and tested type for the bathroom. Laminate bathroom floors are treated against moisture in their backing panels. Some series are even perfectly waterproof and repel water. So, there are no more risks in the bathroom!

Numerous decorations with laminate are possible, you will easily find what suits you: colors, appearance, structures, etc.

Laminate floor maintenance is very simple: simply vacuum or a microfiber mop and you're done.

The carpet: an uncommon bathroom floor

It is certainly surprising, but some types of carpet are compatible with the bathroom! Get informed, because you obviously can't put any type, but the offer exists. The carpet will be treated against humidity to avoid any damage in case of water splashes.

Colors are generally solid

The carpet in the bathroom for a comfortable floor ... Why not? However, pay attention to maintenance! Vacuum regularly for impeccable hygiene!

Cork: the return to the natural

To satisfy your desire for an ecological floor, why not choose a cork floor for the bathroom? Cork is back in fashion and manufacturers have certainly thought about the bathroom option by treating the product against water.

Forget the cork of the 70s! You will now find very refined and imaginative decorations that will in no way give the impression that the floor is made of cork. As with other types of flooring, choose the certified compatible variant well for use in the bathroom.

Plant fiber floor: the natural appearance soft to the touch

Currently, vegetable fiber floors for bathrooms are really taking off. Sisal, reed, coir, jute, these floors offer a surface that may not appeal to everyone, but they certainly look natural. Of all these floors, the maritime rush is to be preferred because it is rot-proof. Ecological and natural, its maintenance is however difficult due to the roughness due to its structure.

Natural stone: luxury under your feet

Natural stone offers unparalleled charm. Expensive but resistant, soap and water are sufficient for maintenance, carefully avoiding aggressive cleaning products.

As an ancient floor, natural stone is known for its longevity and complex laying, which requires suitable skills and tools. Among the most used types of stone, we find:

- granite;
- marble;
- limestone;
- slate;
- local and regional stones (marble from Carrara, Trani, etc.).

However, it should be noted that some stone floors are porous and require a water-repellent treatment for use in damp environments (limestone), while others offer compatible intrinsic characteristics such as granite which, in addition to being very resistant, is also non-slip. Natural stone is offered in slabs, small size tiles and tiles.

Reconstructed stone can offer an interesting alternative given its properties and lower cost.

Waxed concrete: a decidedly modern floor

Waxed concrete lends an industrial character that might not displease contemporary minimalist decorators.

Used as a floor, but also as a coating for walls and furniture, waxed concrete is a cast-on-site concrete loaded with pigments and mineral dust. With a smooth appearance, the waxed concrete is hygienic and the installation is without expansion joints. The waxed concrete chosen as the bathroom floor requires a water-repellent treatment (application of layers of paint).

However, the laying of a waxed concrete can be complex for the layman, as well as the preparation of the substrate. Daily maintenance is carried out with soap and water, but to ensure longevity of the concrete, it may be necessary to renew the application of the water-repellent paint over the years. It should be noted that the waxed concrete in kit has a shorter duration (appearance of micro cracks and cracks already from the first years), compared to the traditional waxed concrete which offers greater durability.

BATHROOM STYLES

What styles for your bathroom?

Glamor or Minimal style? Classic or Ethnic? Mediterranean or Japanese? There are many styles with which

[95]

to create a bathroom and decide, consequently, the bathroom furniture and accessories.

Minimal style bathroom

The style stems from a philosophical current of the 60s, but it kicks off consciously only in the 80s when an attempt is made to react to the diversification of the trends of previous decades with a clear language, immediately recognizable, understandable and shareable by all.

Through a process of simplification, bathroom furniture is reduced to elementary structures to the bare minimum for modern living.

The minimal bathroom is dressed in sober simplicity: suspended geometric shapes and linear surfaces leave the space as free as possible to move, without constraints or impediments.

Minimalism requires the renunciation of decorations, ornaments, accessories, excesses and impractical details. The few pieces of furniture are arranged along the walls in equipped monobloc furniture, mostly suspended from the ground and organized in large drawers.

The shapes of the sanitary ware and bathroom furnishings are clear-cut and defined: pure monolithic and square entities.

For the furnishings and coatings, mostly innovative materials are used: Plexiglas, Corian, glass, resins but also large stoneware slabs.

The surfaces are covered using glossy and lacquered or matt ceramic tiles, they are exclusively in pure shades such as white or gray and in neutral colors, such as earth, ecru and sand. Alternatively, the resin that guarantees smooth surfaces without joints, always in neutral or gray tones.

The bathroom, English style

The English style is inspired by British colors, a fascinating and decidedly vintage style, it is mostly made with a wood paneling, or even with large-format ceramic tiles that imitate lacquered wood.

But a bathroom in this style is also one made with small majolica tiles rich in enamel, rectangular or rhomboid.

The use of English-style sanitary ware and taps is very important, which re-proposes handcrafted ceramic pieces from the 1920s, tall boxes with chains and ceramic knobs.

The bathroom cabinet could be a ceramic sink or a marble console.

To complete the British style, we will also use old trunks, lamps, and British prints.

Oriental style bathroom

The richness of Asian cultures, shapes and materials can be manifested in the bathroom with a profusion of multi-colored, soft and decorated fabrics, in warm and lively colors, such as lacquer red, orange and yellow that match each other on curtains, coverings in wallpaper or carpets, evoking the warmth of oriental countries.

For oriental style bathroom furniture, you can venture into the choice of bathroom furniture from different origins, making use of the charm of unique pieces made by artisans, from Chinese linen holders in lacquered wood to Indian bookcases for bath towels, perforated like lace.

A wooden screen door chiseled in suggestive arabesques, or a brocade puff can add an exotic touch while the preciousness of the finishes such as beaten and chromed metal for the lamps, helps to create an intimate and hospitable place.

Classic style in a modern bathroom

When you hear about classic style, light colors, antique furniture and opulent chandeliers come to mind.

But the concept of classic, from as far back as 450 BC, has continued to change over the course of the various eras, adapting to trends. This is why we speak of classic style, but revisited in a modern key.

The key points of classicism that recall balance, symmetry, harmony and order still represent the foundations on which to rest an environment conceived and designed in a classic style.

The materials used range from the classic marble that covers the bathroom and with which elements such as columns or pilasters are also created. Alternatively, precious mosaics can be used, perhaps with contrasting tones.

Today, for the classic bathroom, porcelain stoneware tiles are available that imitate marble with which to create spectacular floor and wall surfaces, at a cost much lower than that of real marble.

A classic bathroom with shades of beige, dove gray with an important presence of decorations such as the precious mosaic or simply the marked veins of the marble, gray and lapidary or with warm colors and soft lines.

If we think of a classic bathroom in step with the fashions of the moment, we have no doubts: large marble-effect stoneware slabs that completely cover the walls and bathroom furniture of pure elegance.

Mediterranean style bathroom

In the Mediterranean style, white and blue dominate with infinite shades of blue and turquoise.

Amalfi ceramic tiles, glazed and handcrafted decorated, or Sardinian tiles can be used to bring the colors of the sea and the sky into the bathroom.

Even the fabrics must be used in the same colors to make curtains and carpets combined with the coverings.

The white and blue background enhances the beauty of the natural materials with which it combines wonderfully: terracotta, natural wood parquet.

The Mediterranean style is inspired by the white of the lime and the blue of the sea, colors that can also be used for bathroom walls and windows. This style brings the sea wind and salt inside the house.

Modern decorated bathrooms

Usually in the bathroom paintings, photos, drawings are not hung, but what if I wanted to have a particular decoration right on the walls of my bathroom?

It's possible!

The multiple solutions to beautify the walls have led to the affirmation of a real style of furniture.

How to decorate the bathroom?

A brightly colored covering with particular geometries, created with the strangest combinations of shades and decorations. Definitely a courageous choice, but perfect to make the bathroom unique and different from any other. In the large format, to decorate entire walls, we often see customers undecided between the wallpaper and the large decorated slabs. For this reason, we have written an article that explains the characteristics and differences:

Wallpaper or large decorated stoneware slabs?

If, on the other hand, you prefer small formats, the two options we offer the most are mosaics and cement tiles. The mosaic needs no introduction, a decoration par excellence already in ancient Rome. Cement tiles, also known as majolica, have come back into fashion in recent years to cover bathrooms and kitchens.

Wallpaper in the bathroom

Urban Style or metropolitan style bathroom

Do you live in the center and want to bring the style of the city that you see looking out of the window into your home? Or do you live in the country, not by your choice, and want to represent something of your favorite subway directly in your bathroom?

Large-format tiles, which recall a material effect, could be the right choice for a lover of urban style who likes to experiment.

Technical colors that reproduce all shades of gray. A concrete-effect stoneware, large metal-effect slabs or tiles that reproduce the spatula effect of the resin.

It is therefore a question of creating a neutral background that gives continuity to the room, without decorations, if not linear and geometric. In this neutral background, a play of light and shadow is created that gives movement to the environment. In fact, skilfully designed lighting will bring out neutral surfaces.

I leave you other tricks that we use to smooth out the strong visual and emotional impact of these environments:

- ✓ rounded furnishings
- ✓ wood and natural materials, to give warmth
- ✓ contrast with colors and fabrics
- ✓ hang posters and photos instead of paintings
- ✓ the green inside the house is very important for the mood, in these environments it is essential

A strong and truly impactful style, which is very fashionable today!

There are many difficulties in designing industrial-style environments, it is necessary to show imperfections with elegance, being careful not to create cold and unwelcoming environments. Not everyone's choice!

Natural style for the bathroom

This is a type of bathroom in which the furnishings draw inspiration from the shapes of nature and its laws, to adapt as much as possible to man and his needs.

The natural bathroom gives life to interiors where nothing stands in stark contrast and any new element fits in accord with the whole.

The colors and materials are in great harmony and, together, contribute to the general feeling of tranquility. They are modern bathrooms, albeit simple, based on the combination of essentiality and aesthetic pleasure. In addition to wood, it is also possible to use stone, terracotta and bamboo in the bathroom.

Glamor bathroom

The glamorous style, referring to a bathroom, means elegant but also fascinating, almost sensual. The meaning of the word is "charm", but referring to furniture it takes on a meaning of chic, of luxury.

The glamorous pieces of furniture are a mixture of wood, fine leathers and crystal. Usually, the wood is chosen in a dark color (ebony or briar) while for the other materials the colors used are neutrals, added to dark shades of brown and purple.

Table lamps or chandeliers are important protagonists of this style and can be accompanied by details in gold or gilded metal. The ceramic tiles for the bathroom will be of large size and will reproduce precious marbles such as Carrara or Calacatta and perhaps will have inserts in wood-effect stoneware - glossy or matt - of dark color.

BLACK AND WHITE BATHROOM

Black = elegance

White = purity

Black & White = the shades to furnish a bathroom that never goes out of fashion.

The contrasting colors / non-colors par excellence which, together, create environments with a strong character. The surfaces can be covered in ceramic tiles but also in mosaic, marble, Corian. In addition to the black / white contrast, you can also use the contrast between glossy and matt surfaces.

Putting black and white in contrast allows us to create impactful environments

Shabby Chic style bathroom

The Shabby Chic style is adopted by both the world of fashion and furniture. The name literally means "chic-scruffy".

The Country bathroom consists of the worn-elegant dualism of old bathroom furniture recovered and treated to highlight the signs of time.

The pieces of furniture will almost certainly be made using treated woods and repainted in pastel shades of beige, ivory, blue-gray. The style of the bathroom will be a combination of Provencal and retro. The reassuring sensation of "lived-in" comes to life in Victorian-style risers and candelabra, lace and doilies, terracotta, pewter or white ceramic vases.

The ceramic tiles for wall covering can be 20x20 with pastel colors and rural, floral or country decorations. The color of the walls will recall the pastel of the tiles.

The Ethnic style bathroom

This particular style in the bathroom, as the etymology suggests (from the Greek Ethnos = people) was born as a contamination of cultures and traditions from different countries.

An ever-present trend, which manifests itself not only among travel enthusiasts, but in general in an increasing number of admirers, both for the fairly low costs of ethnic bathroom furnishings, and for the extreme versatility and adaptability of this language to any housing situation.

For a long time, the ethnic style was the prerogative of those who had the opportunity to travel a lot and brought back home souvenirs of all kinds.

In recent years, more and more people have seen in ethnicity the possibility of intensely personalizing their home. Furnishing the bathroom in an ethnic style means combining original pieces from Asia, Africa or South America, from furniture to furnishing accessories, from decorations to furnishings, to exotic-inspired furnishings, according to a personal taste that makes suggestive combinations possible.

Thus, referring to the mystery to the evocative power of distant continents, the possibility of recreating atmospheres suspended between meditation and the pleasure of amazement can offer the sensation of having reproduced a distant world in which to take refuge, where to remember places or experiences.

[105]

The surfaces can be covered with decorated Moroccan tiles, or hand-glazed terracotta with an irregular surface. If you want to make the background more neutral, you can use slightly damask decorations. Mosaic can also be used, usually it is multi-colored glazed ceramic mosaic.

The bathroom can also become a small personal wellness center, a private spa. In this case, you will have to choose natural materials (or those that look natural) such as a split stone for the cladding or a wooden decking for the floors.

You can use fabrics such as cotton or, better still, linen using colors ranging from beige to ivory, perhaps with some inserts in coffee color.

As for the bathroom furniture: this will be in wood, while the bathtub can be a whirlpool or it can be wooden. If you prefer to install a shower, you can create a small personal regeneration area, using various water sources.

As usual, lighting is very important and LEDs will be used, perhaps inserted in the vertical surfaces, with the possibility of adjusting (dimming) the intensity but also the color, to obtain a chromotherapy effect.

Also plan to be able to put pots with real plants or, if you want to exaggerate, to prepare a small vertical green wall.

Baroque style bathroom

The Baroque style spread throughout Europe in the 1700s and affected the architecture as well as the furnishings. It stands out for the search for daring decoration, for the richness of the materials and for the magnificence of the final result. This style, which still appeals to Russian or Arab tycoons, is nowadays very little in demand in Italy even if 'Made in Italy', in this sector, boasts several excellent companies.

Even in the bathroom world you can find beautiful furniture, mirrors or accessories in this style.

Classic elegance in the bathroom

The classic style bathroom is inspired by the past and is dressed with elegant, luxurious materials. A classic style bathroom welcomes you like a noble palace and seems to be out of time, timeless.

A classic style bathroom favors precious materials and authentic and refined beauty. In short, it is the opposite of the functional, technological and minimal bathroom.

In the classic bathroom we can find wood used both on the floor and as furniture, preferably walnut wood, but also glass, mirrors, marbles rich in veins and precious materials.

The bathroom furniture is elaborate, refined. Chandeliers and light points are precious, often in hand-worked glass. The mirror frames are elaborate. The taps have shapes and finishes that transform them into small sculptures.

BATHROOM MIRROR LIGHTING: CREATE THE IDEAL LIGHT IN THE WASHBASIN AREA

One of the most important areas of the bathroom undoubtedly corresponds to the mirror and its immediate surroundings. Here people apply make-up, comb their hair, shorten their beards, sometimes get dressed. The mirror therefore needs adequate light, functional to the activities carried out from time to time by guests or tenants at various times of the day. So today we are talking about lamps for the mirror area.

Just any light is not enough, you need an anti-glare device, preferably neutral (not colored), preferably with the possibility of regulation or dimming to ensure maximum comfort and visibility. As for the so-called temperature, i.e. the hue of light expressed in degrees Kelvin (symbol K), the ideal would be a hue between values of around 3,000 K minimum and 4,000 K maximum on a scale that usually ranges from 2,000 K (equivalent to fireplace fire) and 8,000 K (blue sky in summer).

There are thousands of bathroom lights on the market, hundreds of which are specific for the mirror. The choice must therefore be made not only on the basis of these first suggestions, but also in accordance with the furniture and style of the space to be illuminated. Using the same fixture for a contemporary bathroom or a rustic bathroom would make no sense and could lead to unsatisfactory aesthetic results. To help our readers find their way around and avoid unnecessary mistakes, we therefore report as an example 5 lamps selected from the most recent proposals available in Italy. Each embodies a different approach to mirror lighting, with unique and original scenographic effects from which to draw inspiration. Let's start with a classic: the lamp above the mirror.

1. LAMP OVER THE BATHROOM MIRROR

By far one of the favorite solutions for those who want to light up the bathroom mirror. The strong point in this case is the light directed downwards, which hits the mirror in its entirety, concentrating the brightness on the mirror itself and further down to the sink. The lamp model that we would like to recommend is the Skinny LED wall lamp in aluminum and polymethylmethacrylate, a truly original product with the appearance and shape of a shelf of light. The luminaire boasts a consumption of only 28 Watts, ensuring superior energy performance in the face of minimum energy requirements and has the latest generation LED technology called OptiLight. A technology characterized by laser micro-engravings that when turned on allows the light to be distributed uniformly while when turned off it becomes a transparent glass sheet that makes it imperceptible.

2.   LAMP ON THE SIDE OF THE MIRROR

For reasons of aesthetics, personal tastes, height dimensions or for other reasons: the choice of a lamp on the sides of the mirror can depend on many reasons, all equally valid. In this case it is necessary to consider the type of lamp diffuser which must be anti-glare and therefore opaque.

Alternatively, you can opt for adjustable lamps and in this way direct the light where it is needed and make it more comfortable especially at a functional level. Wall lamps, in addition to playing the fundamental role that is to illuminate, are perfect objects or furnishing accessories.

3.   BACKLIT MIRROR WITH SIMPLE LED STRIPS

The third solution that we want to propose is the backlit mirror, it is simply an LED strip applied and positioned behind the mirror to have a diffused light without any encumbrance. This option is suitable for frameless mirrors: it is sufficient to have a space with a depth of only 2 cm to allow the application of the strip. Obviously, we always suggest that the strip be applied inside its aluminum profile useful for dissipation and covered by a diffuser, preferably opaque because it spreads the light evenly. The diffuser also protects the strip from dust, any splashes of water and other similar external agents.

This solution is very often already prepared in the factory with the realization of the mirror with its pros and cons. In the sense that, of course, we have the finished mirror with lighting included, but this does not allow us to choose the type, temperature and quantity of light we want.

4. LIGHTS SUSPENDED FROM THE CEILING TO THE BATHROOM MIRROR

The options indicated so far involve installing a lamp on the bathroom wall, but this is not necessarily the best way. In fact, it is possible to obtain perfect light conditions also thanks to devices that descend from the ceiling, therefore applied at a certain distance from the mirror. The proximity to the reflecting surface will be evaluated according to the model, the size of the lamp, the presence of windows and so on. Surely the ideal height is between 150-175cm to be evaluated also based on our height. This is to avoid unpleasant shadows or reflections that would prevent us from fully enjoying moments of care for ourselves here.

Suspended lamps have become a very popular trend and can be an excellent choice by following the right criteria not only related to the aesthetic side.

5. SPOTLIGHTS AND LED LINES IN THE PRESENCE OF VELETTE AND FALSE CEILINGS

We conclude this roundup of lamps for the bathroom mirror with a special mention. In fact, we are not talking about traditional lamps but about spotlights and LED strips used in the presence of veils and false ceilings above the mirror. If for the strip we refer to the model of point three, for the recessed spotlights the signals are wasted, from the round to the square versions, from the adjustable spotlights to the fixed ones, from the mini fixtures to be placed side by side to the larger ones for a single or double installation. Many opportunities for one goal: to make the most of your bathroom without spending a fortune and consuming precious energy!

THINGS TO KNOW TO CHOOSE THE PAINT FOR THE BATHROOM

The bathroom is the room in the house that needs the most protection and hygiene. Since this is a room particularly subject to humidity, it must be painted with a bathroom paint that cannot be attacked by mold, capable of avoiding the settlement of micro-organisms and resisting jets of water on the walls without getting damaged, while ensuring an aesthetically pleasing result.

High humidity and direct water jets can cause problems on bathroom walls. Here's how to preserve the appearance and healthiness of these environments over time, with the right paints.

Use Breathable Paints to Avoid Mold Formation

To think that vapor passes systematically from the inside to the outside is a mistake. In particularly humid environments such as bathrooms, the high level of humidity, poor ventilation and infrequent air exchange create the conditions for condensation to form. The external walls of the bathroom are more prone to this phenomenon as they have a lower temperature. For example, after a shower the bathroom temperature is about 23C with humidity at 70%. Near the surface of the outer wall the temperature decreases and the humidity increases. By using the psychrometric diagram it's estimated that, if on the surface of the wall the temperature is 12C, the air reaches saturation point (100% humidity) and therefore there is the formation of condensation, which in the long run can cause a proliferation of molds, these are, in fact, the main causes of the onset of mold.

One of the thermal insulation systems can be a good solution to prevent the problem, contributing to improving the performance of the walls and to increase the temperature of the internal parts, and consequently decreasing the risk of condensation formation.

If the thermal insulation is not present, to limit this phenomenon, unsightly but especially hazardous to your health, you need to use breathable paint with high diffusivity into water vapor.

Paint the ceiling and walls with a thermal effect paint

In choosing the paint for bathroom we tend to consider only the aesthetic effect on the walls, but in reality, the ceilings are an important element, the mildew is formed precisely in the top corners, in correspondence of the structural thermal bridges. For this reason, it is good to choose a washable anti-condensation paint with a thermal effect. This interior painting is the evolution of traditional paints and is the result of scrupulous technological research. Thanks to special thermoreflective fillers, and elements that combat surface condensation in the colder areas of the environment and in addition to the protective effect, this painting improves the living comfort ensuring a feeling of warmth, even to the touch.

The walls of the bathroom can be protected with an anti-mold treatment.

In the case of mildew already being present, it is important to follow the right process of reorganization, before applying the new paint, by acting in this way: Apply a sanitized disinfectant on the mold and surrounding areas, in order to eliminate the microflora, after leaving to act for 24 hours cover the walls with a paint for broad-spectrum interior. In modern houses it is more and more common to use decorative paints, creating a play of colors on the walls that become furnishing elements. Here, you are influencing also the finish of the bathroom, where more and more often paint in used in place of ceramic tiles.

Cover the old tiles with a water-based enamel

Even to renew the bathroom quickly and easily, without masonry works, painting directly on the tiles can cover the ceramic to give a new look to the bathroom, and at the same time create condensation protection.

The solutions for painting the bathroom are countless and allow you to combine aesthetic and functional needs, while ensuring maximum protection of the walls.

HOW TO PAINT THE BATHROOM

Usually, the bathroom is one of the smallest rooms in the house, therefore easier to paint... but only in appearance: the constant presence of water in this room can in fact cause some problems. That's why painting your bathroom is a job to be done with extreme care and diligence. Then follow our tips to make no mistake!

What it takes to paint at home

1) Choose the colors to use and the finish of the paint

For bathroom walls we recommend choosing a semi-gloss finish, to solve the frequent problems of humidity and cleaning that are common in this space.

There is a line of kitchen and bathroom paints specially formulated to provide optimum performance in high humidity conditions. Using advanced technologies, these high-quality paints are designed to withstand frequent washing and maintain the beauty of their finish. They resist stains well, are particularly bright and... you can also use them to paint bathroom cabinets!

2) prepare the room

Remove ceiling lights, lamps, and accessories from the ceiling, as well as any shelving and any appliances present. Remove the electrical outlet covers, keeping all screws and fasteners together in a plastic bag. Tape a small plastic bag around the knobs and any objects you can't remove.

Cover the floors with plastic or, even better, fabric sheets. Apply the paper tape along the baseboards and jambs that are not to be painted. Remember to remove the tape when the paint is still wet.

Use a scraper to remove old peeling paint and be sure to wear safety glasses to prevent paint chips from getting into your eyes. Fill cracks and holes with putty, wait for it to dry and… start painting!

3) painting walls and ceilings

First, paint the ceiling. Using a roller attached to an extension rod, run the paint in one direction, moving quickly to keep the edge wet and avoid excess pressure. If you need to take a break from your painting project, instead of rinsing out the brush or roller, wrap it carefully in plastic wrap (classic kitchen wrap is fine too) or an airtight plastic bag. You can also leave it there overnight: the plastic wrap will keep the paint wet, so the roller can be reused safely even after a few hours, then proceed with the walls.

Once the work is finished, do not throw away the rollers and brushes, with proper cleaning and storage, you can reuse these precious painting tools many times. Reusing them saves you time and money!

HOW TO CHOOSE THE BEST SHOWER ENCLOSURE

Those who have not yet decided, or have not been able, to abandon the classic shower curtains, in this chapter will find tips on how to choose the best shower enclosure. The traditional curtain, which still represents the solution for many homes, has in fact very specific limits: the risk is that of never completely protecting the bathroom from splashes and water coming from the shower. Modern shower enclosures, on the

other hand, represent an absolutely safe solution from this point of view and beyond. In the examples that we will see, in fact, we will understand together how to choose the best shower enclosure, equipped with glass, crystal or plastic panels, with the best equipment also from the point of view of the shower tray, another fundamental element in choosing the best shower enclosure.

1. Evaluate all options

Before choosing the best shower enclosure, it will be good to focus on the options available on the market. The range of materials on the market, in fact, goes from glass to crystal, to resin solutions, capable of adapting to any type of environment and situation. To be evaluated, to choose the best shower enclosure, based on the architectural configuration of the space. Looking at both the quality and the design of the shower enclosure, to choose the best and most suitable one for your space.

2. Assess individual needs

In choosing the best shower cubicle, the needs of the bathroom in which the shower cubicle will be inserted must be taken into account. Understanding, therefore, based on the needs of use, what problems and advantages the choice may have over use. In case, for example, of continuous and repeated use, it will be better to opt for solutions that are easy to clean and resistant to both the stresses of use and those due to cleaning.

3. The space around the shower

To choose the best shower enclosure for your bathroom, another fundamental element is the architectural configuration of the space, the volumes available, the location of the drains. And from the materials that you intend to use for the rest of the bathroom furniture. Solutions with transparent pvc panels with a sinuous shape, in fact allow not to close the configuration of the space, helping to keep it airy and bright.

4. The versatility of sliding doors

In choosing the best shower enclosure it is good to consider the great versatility guaranteed by sliding doors, the ideal solution for small bathrooms, where it is necessary to make the most of every available centimeter. A shower enclosure in fact, must have excellent access and closure, thanks to sliding doors that overlap the fixed panels during opening.

5. The evolution of shower enclosures with sliding doors

If the sliding doors of the shower enclosures represent one of the aspects to be evaluated in choosing the best shower enclosure, their evolution has improved their use and the possibilities of simple and effective cleaning. The technology, in fact, makes it possible to avoid superstructures in materials such as aluminum, which were difficult to clean and subject to deterioration due to use which made them not very durable. To choose the best shower enclosure, therefore, it will be good to also look at these details of the structures.

6. Hinged doors to the shower enclosure

However, solutions with sliding doors and panels are not the only ones. Indeed, the doors for the hinged shower enclosure represent an excellent alternative, especially in certain architectural situations. In this case, the space available must be greater, to allow you to open and close the shower in a comfortable and functional way.

7. A fixed shower cubicle

Among the options to be evaluated in choosing the best shower enclosure, that of a fixed structure must be carefully evaluated. If the space of the bathroom allows it, in fact, the solution of a fixed shower box represents an excellent alternative: it allows greater integration into the environment and limits the need for panels, gaskets and doors.

8. Alternative solutions

Among the alternative solutions to the classic shower enclosure, if the architectural structure of the space allows it, you can opt for a protection consisting of a thin wall, which does not necessarily, as we can see, reach from floor to ceiling.

9. Protection up to the ceiling

In the case we see, however, the shower box consists of a fixed structure that reaches from the floor to the ceiling, as if it were a separation wall. A very interesting solution from the point of view of decoration, but also practical and safe in terms of functionality.

10. Different finishes

If the choice of the best shower box must take into account the materials that make up the main structure, the finishes can become a way to enrich the structure. In the case we see, inside the shower we find a mirror wall, very useful for enlarging the space, giving it unexpected perspectives and dimensions.

11. Creative solutions

Also, in terms of design, the latest generation materials and techniques allow great versatility, widening the field to different shapes and colors. As in the case we see, with a shower enclosure with orange and transparent surfaces, of great yield from an aesthetic point of view.

SMALL BATHROOM? HERE ARE THE MOST SUITABLE AND FUNCTIONAL SPACE-SAVING SHOWER ENCLOSURES

When the dimensions of the bathroom are limited, or in the event that an already installed shower tray is small, the shower cubicle must be carefully studied so that it is equally functional and comfortable, with reference to both the internal space and the size of the opening doors.

1. Small showers: but how small?

The definition of "small bathroom", and consequently of "small shower", could be subjective and vary greatly depending on the build of the homeowner.

With reference to the contemporary dimensions of houses, bathrooms and showers, we could therefore distinguish between:

- very small shower: 70 x 70 cm. A fairly common size of shower tray until a few decades ago, today really rare (and which we do not recommend, in fact it is very difficult to move and wash in such a space).

- small shower: 80 x 80 cm. Although not very comfortable, an 80 cm square shower can be a solution for mini bathrooms, secondary or service bathrooms, bathrooms in holiday homes or attics. If possible, it would still be preferable, to move with greater ease, to add about ten centimeters at least on one of the two sides.

[125]

● standard shower: 70 x 90 cm. One of the most popular dishes in today's apartments: it is an average size, comfortable enough to move around inside the shower box. But 80 x 90 cm could be easier.

● large shower: from 90 x 90 cm the shower area becomes comfortable enough for a person of average build. For example, there are 80 x 100 cm or 90 x 120 cm shower trays on the market that allow you to create a very spacious and airy shower area.

In this chapter, therefore, we consider shower closures suitable for dishes of maximum size 80 x 90 cm.

2. Small showers: which closures to choose?

When the shower is really small you need to be careful of 2 things:

● the entrance space to the shower;

● the external (and internal) dimensions of the doors.

The entrance space is important when considering shower enclosures with sliding doors: an 80 x 80 cm shower enclosure, for example, has limited entry space considering the size of the fixed doors and the overlap # of the sliding ones.

[# we talk about overlapping if the sliding door does not perfectly overlap the fixed door when the shower box is completely open: the central opening space loses a few centimeters.]

The external dimensions of the doors must be considered above all in relation to the surrounding furnishings and sanitary ware. If the bathroom is small, in fact, it is likely that they are located a few centimeters from the shower itself.

Which shower solutions for small bathrooms are therefore more functional?

• The shower enclosure with sliding doors is comfortable enough for standard size plates (70 x 90 cm for example), but it is good to inquire about the entrance space by consulting the technical data sheets of the models (depending on the dimensions of the profiles and the sliding system the overlap of the doors can steal a few centimeters). With such models, therefore, you enter / exit the corner of the shower box.

• If you prefer to access the shower from one of the two sides, on the other hand, you can consider installing a combined fixed door shower enclosure, which must be chosen based on how much it can clutter externally. For example, for a swing door to fully open, there must be nothing in front of the shower. A door with two saloon doors, on the other hand, halves the external dimensions of the glass and gives the possibility to open the doors also towards the inside of the shower box.

A closure consisting of a fixed piece of glass and an opening door could be an aesthetic and functional compromise, as could a convenient folding door (also called a folding door).

The same reasoning applies when the shower enclosure closes a niche.

● A small bathroom with a walk-in shower (i.e. with an open space, without a door), on the other hand, is conceivable only if inside it is possible to obtain a shower space with a minimum size of 80/90 x 140/150 cm, which allows for a comfortable entrance space and a fixed glass of sufficient size to avoid too many outwards splashes. Maybe you will sacrifice space for the bathroom cabinet or eliminate the bidet (in the case of a second bathroom this could be an option to consider).

● Finally, a note about small corner showers: in principle the semicircular shower enclosure takes up more (internal) space than a rectangular model of the same size. To be evaluated therefore when the space in the bathroom is really limited. In addition to the version with 2 fixed and 2 sliding doors, there is the one with two single doors, which makes entry easier.

The last element not to be overlooked for small showers is the presence or absence of a frame: shower enclosures without profiles are aesthetically lighter and therefore more suitable for small bathrooms.

TYPES OF SHOWER ENCLOSURE OPENINGS

Hinged, folding or sliding: there are different types of shower box openings, so how to choose the one that best suits your bathroom? In this article we at Acquistaboxdoccia.it want to give you a useful explanation on the pros and cons of the various types of doors, to guide you towards the best purchase.

In fact, when you decide to buy a shower enclosure, there are many variables to take into consideration: the dimensions and materials you prefer, the style needs, as well as the right quality / price ratio, but the most important of all is precisely its opening system, of which we illustrate the main features below.

SLIDING

It is the ideal solution for small bathrooms to optimize the available space and is also recommended for floor-level installations; among its advantages we find the particular tightness, with the water that does not come out towards the outside and a space-saving opening, its only negative point could be the difficulty of cleaning the wheels on the tracks and the overlapping of the profiles.

SWING

This type of opening is easier to clean and moreover it is very pleasing to the eye, even if the overall dimensions of the frame remain with the relative reduction of the opening and the risk, albeit minimal, of water leaks if the lower frame is not inserted.

BOOK / BELLOWS

The folding / folding opening model has folding doors which, on the one hand, reduce the space inside the shower cubicle, on the other can be considered an excellent response to small bathrooms.

In addition to these factors, it will also be good to consider the compatibility of the shower door with the type of design with which you have chosen to furnish your home, which can be more classic or modern by also choosing the glass processing of the doors: transparent, satin or with details like serigraphs.

A golden rule to keep in mind when you are going to buy a shower enclosure: remember to take the measurements and communicate them to the store in order to avoid finding yourself in difficulty at the time of assembly.

Shower area: Is it better to have a hinged or sliding door shower?

The shower area is a fundamental place in a home, where a person can cool off and relax, especially after a tiring and intense working day. Compared to the classic bathtub, which is open to the rest of the room, the shower box is characterized by a completely closed space, which allows you to avoid wetting outside and excessively clutter.

Surely, it is the ideal choice for medium and small bathrooms. They can be formed in many different types of structure, also based on the size and space required, but certainly the most popular shower enclosures are hinged and sliding doors.

Let's see the main differences between the two, and which one should be mounted in your bathroom.

The shower area with hinged door box

The hinged door opening and closing system is the classic one of all doors in the house, that is, with the door that opens outwards with a push or pull.

As for the use of this system for shower enclosures, there are several advantages that certainly bring:

Very aesthetically beautiful for your bathroom, they adapt perfectly to the interior design;

Shower stalls often tend to get dirty over time. Thanks to the hinged door, cleaning it is very easy, as it is enough to open it from the outside and clean it with the various special products. This allows a much more comfortable cleaning of the sliding door, which we will see later;

Generally, in this type of system there is no lower frame, and it allows to avoid the accumulation of hair and other residues;

Wider entry space than all other models. These are the main advantages of a hinged door shower enclosure and are good to keep in mind when buying a new shower enclosure. Unfortunately, in response to the positive factors there are also consequent negative factors, namely:

The clutter that the swing door creates is certainly evident, and therefore this aspect must be considered when

[131]

building the shower area. Having furniture, bathroom fixtures or anything else nearby is not convenient;

It is true that hinged doors do not have a frame, and it is useful to avoid accumulations, but there is a risk that they cause the water to escape underneath;

The water droplets that obviously accumulate on the door while taking a shower tend to drip outwards and not inwards.

The shower area with sliding door box

This type of shower box is obviously aesthetically different from the previous one, but it is particularly convenient for very small bathrooms, where it is also necessary to put appliances, such as washing machine, dryer or simply where the arrangement of the sanitary fixtures does not allow a hinged opening.

The main advantages of sliding door shower areas are:

They require very small dimensions, and therefore take up less space, since the door must not be opened towards the outside;

The droplets that are created do not escape outside but fall inside, without wetting outside;

This structure has better insulating and hermetic properties, thanks also to the underlying frame that prevents water from escaping.

Obviously, also in this case, this type of structure of the shower box brings both advantages, as seen, but also negative aspects. In particular:

The presence of the frame is not aesthetically beautiful and it is also necessary to clean it often, as it causes various residues to accumulate over time;

It is not completely comfortable, as the entry and exit space will never be complete, considering the fixed glass part, the various welds etc;

It is very difficult to clean, as it must be done internally in a usually quite small space. Furthermore, this is made even more difficult if the glass doors are overlapped.

Hinged or sliding, which shower box to choose?

We have seen all the strengths and weaknesses of the two main types of opening and closing the shower cubicles. So, which one should you choose?

The answer is: it depends. When you are designing your new shower area, it is essential to carefully analyze every single aspect, positive and negative, of a cubicle system.

If you have a large bathroom and are looking for a refined and elegant solution, the swing door shower enclosure is ideal, while in the case of small bathrooms with little space the optimal solution is a sliding door shower enclosure.

In each case we advise you to always choose a shower box with 6 or better 8mm thick crystals which are respectively the mid-range and the top of the sector.

WALK IN SHOWER: ADVANTAGES AND DISADVANTAGES

The shower is a fundamental element of the home. Over time, due to the great importance it has, the shower has undergone various evolutions in technique, use and design. The last of these is the walk-in shower, which completely revises the classic structure we are used to, re-proposing it in a minimal key.

Walk in shower: a new shower concept

In another article, we happened to talk about "Bathtubs with showers: a single solution for multiple needs". Today we talk about the walk-in shower, another fundamental element of the bathroom.

In the classic case, we are used to seeing a well-defined ceramic shower tray, with marked edges and a consistent height. On this, the closing glass plates or the sliding curtains are placed to ensure the closing of the shower box and to prevent the escape of water coming from the diffuser. It is significant to think of the fact that we are always used to talking about the shower enclosure, precisely because we imagine in our mind a space closed in on itself and different from the rest of the bathroom.

[135]

In walk-in evolution, as the English name itself suggests, we no longer have to open swing doors or curtains, enter and close them behind us.

The walk-in is in fact normally without at least one wall. That is to say that if we want to obtain it in a corner, then it is necessary to position a single glass plate in order to guarantee a single diaphragm but leaving one of the four sides open. From here you can guess the definition walk in, that is a space in which you simply enter by walking.

We can even put the walk in on one of the four sides of the bathroom, place a single glass in the center and leave two entrances free on the sides.

Under the banner of contemporary design, we will install a minimal glass, with essential lines and possibly without a frame.

Focusing now on the shower tray, which is also in line with the dematerialization process of the cabin and the glass, it simplifies, following a cleaner and simpler design. Even in some walk-in showers the ceramic plate no longer exists, but the space is obtained on the floor itself by making a cut in the tiles under which the water drain is placed.

What are the advantages of walk-in showers and what are the disadvantages? Let's list them below to evaluate them thoroughly.

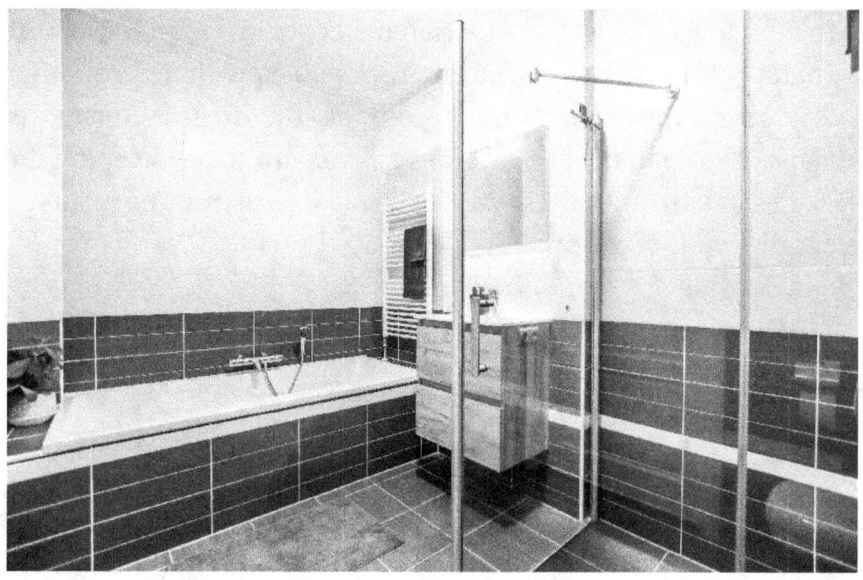

The advantages of walk-in showers:

The design is certainly more captivating and modern, the space of the bathroom and of the open shower are freed by being placed in direct communication with each other and the cleaning of this shower is easier and more immediate, since the surfaces are more minimal, without folds, hinges, seals.

The disadvantages of walk-in showers:

Since one of the four sides is missing, you will understand the water splash problem for yourself. This requires one of the two shower sizes to be quite substantial, around 120cm or more.

As the cabin no longer exists, you are in direct contact with the bathroom environment and therefore suffer more from the sensation of cold as the steam constantly escapes, while in the classic shower it accumulates, keeping the box rather warm. In these cases, a heat source must be installed near the walk-in point.

Walk-in ideal size

From what has been explained so far, it is easy to understand that the dimensions of walk-in showers require more significant measures than closed solutions. Both to avoid splashes, and to avoid water leaks from below, and to guarantee the opening and fluidity effect typical of this type of shower. For this reason, we advise against sizing the long side less than 120 cm, and the optimal is 150-160 cm or more.

Finally, what are the prices for the purchase of this type of shower?

Sometimes less than a normal shower. In fact, it is true that the box does not exist as we are used to normally understanding it. What remains is the plate, which as we have seen we can also not install, and at least one perimeter glass plate. So, you can also spend 200 or 300 dollars less than normal, but many other factors can make the difference! In fact, if you think about it, there are cheap ceramic shower trays from 110 dollars and others in Corian that can cost several hundred dollars. Furthermore, if you want a great impact effect, you could choose quality brass or steel taps and the price could go up to 200 dollars for the components alone.

HOW TO ASSEMBLE A SHOWER ENCLOSURE

Find out how to assemble a new shower enclosure step by step, from tools to assembly tips, and give yourself a corner of complete well-being!

Tired of flooding the whole bathroom every time you take a shower with the classic curtain let's face it, as ugly as it is uncomfortable? Perhaps the time has come to buy a shower box: a minimal expense that will change the face of your bathroom and transform the shower into a moment of true relaxation.

If you have a minimum of manual skills you can, in a few simple steps, assemble your shower cubicle yourself and further reduce costs.

The first thing to do is to take the measurements of your shower tray and then buy a suitable box. There are countless models on the market, made in different materials and sizes.

Let's see how to take the measurements for the different types of shower trays:

Square or rectangular shower tray in niche: it is therefore a shower surface with only one free side, the measurement must be made from tile to tile, just above the shower tray.

Square or rectangular corner shower tray: this type of shower tray has two free sides and the measurement is taken from the wall to the outer edge of the tray.

Square or rectangular wall-mounted shower tray: in this case the shower surface has 3 free sides, the measurement is carried out between the two external edges and between the tiled wall and the front edge of the shower.

Oversized curved shower tray: in this case we do not recommend taking the measurement directly from the shower enclosure, as it is difficult to calculate the exact angle of curvature. A reliable way is to use a cardboard template on which to trace and then cut out the perimeter of the shower box.

For assembly you will need:

- New shower box
- Drill with ceramic tips
- Screwdrivers
- Dowels
- Screws
- Meter
- Spirit level
- Transparent silicone

Here are the steps to take to assemble your new shower enclosure:

1. First, carefully wash the shower surface, removing any traces of dirt and carefully dry the surface (In this way the silicone you will put on later will have a perfect seal).
2. Once the surface has dried, take the profiles of the shower box and place them on the walls, with the help of an indelible marker, draw small marks in correspondence with the holes (both on the shower surface and on the wall). To avoid making mistakes, help yourself with a spirit level.
3. Drill holes on the traces left with the marker. Proceed very carefully, use only tips suitable for ceramic avoiding the formation of cracks that would irreparably damage the surfaces.
4. Once the holes have been made, fix the shower enclosure profiles by inserting the plugs with the respective screws.
5. Using the supplied connectors, join the vertical profiles with the horizontal ones and fasten everything with screws.
6. At this point you can insert the movable walls, sliding them in the appropriate tracks on the profiles.
7. After mounting the walls, proceed with closing the corners, using the L-connectors supplied.
8. At this point all that remains is to seal the frame with silicone (this last step is very important because it prevents the formation of annoying water infiltrations and unsanitary molds).
9. Let the silicone dry for at least 8 hours.
10. Once the silicone is perfectly dry, you just have to take a nice hot shower!

HOW TO CHOOSE A BATHTUB FOR YOUR HOME

The bathroom in a home cannot be considered complete without a bathtub, an object that was once considered an accessory, but which today has returned to being the center of furniture.

Whether it's a traditional bathroom or a home spa, choosing the right bathtub is not easy.

On the market you can find many models, which meet different needs of use, space and budget. The best bathtubs address your specific needs, and the room you will need to fix.

To understand which bathtub to buy, follow this short guide, and find out which are the features to consider and which are all the models to choose from.

Bathtubs according to shape

One of the first things to consider when buying a bathtub is the shape. This must adapt to your bathroom, both in terms of available space and style of furniture.

Each bathroom style has an ideally shaped bathtub, be it a classic, modern, industrial, romantic bathroom, and so on.

The rectangular bathtub is one of the most traditional models, and also one of the most popular. It can be placed in practically any type of bathroom, and can also be adapted to the smallest corners of the room. The rectangular models can start from a minimum of 100cm up to tanks that are even two meters long.

The oval bathtub is elegant and romantic. It fits very well in both modern and classic contexts, depending on the model. Unlike the rectangular bathtub, however, it does not fit on the wall, and therefore requires a bathroom with larger spaces.

The corner bathtub is the best for small spaces, because it mixes functionality with aesthetics. While they may be smaller in size, they are usually quite deep. The deep pools offer better immersion and are very popular. A separate type of tub is the asymmetrical one: these are tubs with particular shapes, which can mix corners with curves, and are usually real design pieces. Those that have rectangular sides can be installed on the wall.

Bathtubs according to the material

Bathtubs can be produced with different types of materials, each one satisfying specific need. From the economic ones, to the valuable ones, there is the right material for everyone.

The most used materials for bathtubs are acrylic, resin, marble resin, enameled steel and enameled cast iron.

Acrylic is one of the most popular materials for bathtubs. It is durable, non-slip, antibacterial, and relatively inexpensive. Handling acrylic is simple, but still requires regular cleaning.

Resin is another popular material because it is malleable and flexible, and can be requested in different colors. It is very durable and can be repaired in case of damage, as well as being non-slip. Resin maintenance requires the use of mildly aggressive detergents.

Marble resin is a product that contains resin and minerals. It is an eco-friendly material because it can be recycled. It is resistant, antibacterial and can be cleaned easily. Also, in this case, the material can be customized, creating a pleasant effect similar to marble (hence its name).

Enameled steel is the ideal material to withstand different water temperatures. It is very resistant, but the enamel that covers it must be thick and of good quality, otherwise the surface will be damaged.

Enameled cast iron is another resistant material, both to shocks and temperatures. It has the advantage of retaining the heat of the hot water, thus making bathing more pleasant. It is a particular material, especially loved for vintage models.

Bathtubs by size

Another element that must absolutely be kept in mind is the size of the tub. Whether it is a built-in bathtub, a free-standing or a paneled bathtub, it is always necessary to understand what the dimensions of the bathroom are and what space to dedicate to the bathtub.

Our advice is not to sacrifice too much space for the bathtub, even if you want a very large and comfortable bathtub.

[144]

The risk is that there is not enough space for the rest of the bathroom fixtures. To overcome the problem of the small bathroom, you can use a corner bathtub, deep but adapted to the available space. Alternatively, if you have a very large bathroom, you can choose a splendid free-standing bathtub, both in the classic rectangular shape and in the much-loved oval one. The free-standing designer bathtubs are an accessory that will make the environment much more sophisticated, and your bathrooms much more relaxing.

Bathtubs by style

We have already mentioned, previously, how the style of the tub should be consistent with the rest of the furniture.

For example, a large oval free-standing bathtub fits well in a classic or romantic decor with soft and warm colors. A classic rectangular bathtub, perhaps built-in, is perfect for a modern bathroom without too many frills. A designer bathtub, with asymmetrical shapes, is perfect for a minimal bathroom with solid colors. Color also plays a certain role in the style of the bathroom. The classic color of the bathtub is pearly white, but there are some models that allow you to choose between other colors as well. For example, a bathtub can be entirely black, or steel-colored for a modern and avant-garde effect.

HOW TO ALIGN THE WALLS IN THE BATHROOM WITH PLASTER

In the decoration of the bathroom walls, the main material is the tile. And for tiles, the evenness of the surface is very important. We will figure out how to align the walls in the bathroom, in which case they need to be leveled, when you can get by with small ones, and when you need to apply plaster.

When should I align the bathroom walls?

Before tiling the walls, it is necessary to study them for flatness, vertically and horizontally.

It is necessary to apply plaster in cases where there are significant differences in level in all directions or the wall has an irregular shape (concavity, "belly").

To assess the real need for plaster, you must evaluate the following parameters:

Often the problem is not even in the walls themselves, but in the corners. The angles should be even, 90 degrees. Otherwise, the tiles will not fit evenly into the bathroom, and the furniture with the bathroom will not rise evenly. It is mainly because of the corners that the plastering must be done.

Verification is done using a building level, rail, plumb line, measuring tape, or using a laser level. All these tools allow you to accurately determine the accuracy of the finish and assess the need for drastic measures. In cases where tiles are to be laid on the walls, the level differences must not exceed 1 cm. If the value is greater, it will be noticeable visually while small irregularities with a generally flat wall, usually form in case of removal of old tiles and small indentations, roughness, protrusions can remain on the rough surface. Such irregularities are not critical, so you can do it easier, using a simple spatula.

In any case, it is important to check the uniformity of the walls as a whole, perhaps due to a previous repair that was not carried out well and without taking into account the problems with the corners of the walls.

The irregularities of the spots in some parts of the wall are easily fixed with putty. Usually, the imperfections of the wall are covered with a solution of tile glue, a small layer of it is applied, enough to hide the crack, after which it is necessary to wait 24 hours (the applied layer must be completely dry). At the end of the day, you can proceed directly to laying the tiles.

What if it was necessary to plaster the walls?

If the bathroom walls are in a rough state then obviously you will have to plaster them. Gypsum mixtures are used for differences of more than 1-1.5 cm, the main task here is to correctly set the floors to avoid an increase in plaster consumption, a thickness of more than 1 cm is quite expensive.

The main advantage of plaster over drywall is space saving. The walls are sometimes easier to level with drywall, but in this case the frame and the sheets themselves "steal" a significant part of the bathroom area.

Before starting the process of applying the finished solution, the walls should be cleaned of dust, dirt, oil stains, which will reduce the level of adhesion.

How to plaster the bathroom walls?

When plastering the walls in the bathroom, it is very important to consider the operational characteristics of the room. The bathroom is an area of high humidity, with frequent temperature changes, condensation. Therefore, it is important to choose the appropriate type of plaster that can withstand such harsh conditions.

First of all, the walls must be treated with a hydrophobic base. This composition will strengthen the adhesion of the wall to the plaster and form a barrier to the development of fungi and bacteria.

The choice of plaster depends on the material of the rough base. For plastering concrete and brick walls, it is advisable to give preference to moisture-resistant cement compounds, while if laid out from gypsum blocks, the mixture should be gypsum.

The only room in the apartment where the owners think less about the material for the wall covering is a bathroom. In 9 out of 10 cases, these are ceramic tiles, more suitable for difficult operating conditions: high humidity and sudden changes in temperature. Alternatively, paint, PVC panels or waterproof wallpaper can be used. At the same time, the laying, painting and wallpapering of the tiles are impossible without preparatory work, among which the alignment of the bathroom walls.

There are two reasons for leveling the wall:

aesthetics - finishing on a flat wall looks neat, does not spoil the overall impression of the interior of the apartment;

technical - associated with the risk of voids forming under the tile when drying the adhesive. At any time in such places, the lining material can be damaged. A second scenario is possible: the reduction, the adhesive mass drags the individual tiles together, interrupting the harmony of the laid tiles.

Therefore, the procedure for leveling the walls is a mandatory step in the decoration of the bathroom, which can be done by several methods:

The easiest and most convenient way to level the walls is to use drywall, not ordinary, but resistant to moisture. The method has many advantages:

- the alignment process takes several hours;
- technology does not require special knowledge and experience - the work is done by hand;
- significant defects can be hidden;

Among the cons:

✓ drywall does not do well in areas with high humidity: near the shower and above the sink. It is necessary to use plaster;
✓ the installation of gypsum significantly reduces the useful area of the bathroom - at least 3 cm on each side;
✓ in many cases waterproofing work is required.

Another classic way of leveling walls is applying plaster, which has many positive aspects:

✓ It is possible to obtain a perfectly smooth surface;
✓ after drying, the wall is ready to withstand any mechanical stress;
✓ indispensable in wet rooms;
✓ holds any tile, including porcelain stoneware;
✓ the area of the room is practically not reduced;
✓ consumables (cement and sand) are not very expensive.

The method also has drawbacks:

✓ in the presence of unevenness of more than 3 cm, a large amount of materials will be required, significantly increasing costs;
✓ technology is complex, it requires skills;
✓ the process takes several days.

Requirements for the surface of the bathroom walls

Some materials require a perfectly smooth surface, while others generally reduce the preparatory work for removing mold.

Tile laying specialists often encounter a situation where the bathroom walls were not aligned with the tiles: the height differences were compensated for by the tile adhesive. The results of this work appear very quickly: the glue shrinks when it dries (the shrinkage of the adhesive layer by 5 cm reaches 1 cm). What happens to the tile is not difficult to guess: it breaks or peels off.

However, perfectly even walls are not required for laying the tiles. With a height difference of 1cm, the adhesive will be fine. The exception is mosaic tiles which need a smooth wall. The explanation is simple: in any case, the adhesive shrinks. Under standard tiles it is unnoticeable. Under the surface mosaic, all irregularities become immediately visible.

Pvc panels

The only finishing material that does not respond to the curvature of the walls is the polyvinyl chloride panels. The plastic furniture manages to hide any errors and defects. Here, preparation for finishing work comes down to repairing cracks and holes, as well as removing mold.

color

Recently, the fashion for painting bathroom walls has returned. Under the paint layer, any irregularities - elevations, bumps, cracks on the surface of the walls become immediately visible. Therefore, before painting the bathroom, it is necessary to bring the surface of its walls in perfect condition.

Wall alignment instructions

There are two ways to level the walls: plastering or using drywall. Each of them has its strengths and weaknesses, and as for the bathroom, there are several clarifying points:

1. It is better to plaster under the wall tiles. The small area of the plaster and the 1 cm bending tolerance allow you to perform the work yourself even in the absence of experience.

In extreme cases, if there is still no necessary plan, the wall can be puttied, smoothing out the mistakes made. The alignment of the walls in the bathroom with the drywall under the tile is justified only when the plane is blocked by more than 2.5 cm.

2. It is better to use drywall if you want to paint, it allows you to get perfectly even walls. If the curvature of the surface is small, you can do without a frame and glue panel directly to the walls. With significant curvature, in any case, you will need to install the case and line it with a gyroscope.

Owners of apartments dealing with plasterboard, will easily understand how to align the walls in the bathroom with this material. For those who are faced with plasterboard wall sheathing for the first time, we will see the whole process step by step.

In practice, two methods are used to level the walls with drywall:

✓ without frame;
✓ with a crate.

[154]

Without frame. Using this method, existing types of glue and technology allow you to align the wall with a curvature of up to 4 cm, but only for wallpaper or paint. A thick layer of glue does not hold the tile, which must be taken into account (tiling on drywall is done with a thickness of adhesive mass of not more than 1 cm).

Step 1 The wall is cleaned of dirt, old plaster and mold. All types of niches are leveled with putty. Using a plumb line and a level, the curvature of the wall is determined. If it does not exceed 1.5 cm, the panel is glued directly to the wall.

Step 2 The drywall is primed and then suspended. Planks are attached to the sides of adjacent walls to control vertical and a line is drawn in chalk for horizontal alignment on the floor. Sheets of drywall are cut to the size of the wall.

Step 3 The sheet is applied to the wall and aligned in the horizontal and vertical plane (a level is required). You can change the drywall plan only by pressing it against the wall. Pulling inside the bathroom does not work - the foam (glue) is not rubber, it is not pulled out.

Step 4 After the glue dries, the drywall surface is treated with a primer and the joints are sealed. After a day, the surface of the plasterboard can be plastered.

If the curvature of the surface exceeds 1.5 cm, the gaskets will help. For this, the places with the largest curve inside the wall are determined. The frame strips are placed on the wall, and then drywall is glued. The use of polyurethane foam as an adhesive mass is excluded. It is recommended to use ready-made putty.

With a crate.

The large curvature of the walls requires the installation of a batten. The work is carried out in the following sequence:

- ✓ the wall is hung to determine the mounting points of the guide profile;
- ✓ the passage points of the ceiling profile are determined;
- ✓ suspensions are attached to the profile line;
- ✓ holes for dowels are drilled in the floor and ceiling;
- ✓ all types of profile are cut with a grinder or a hacksaw for metal;
- ✓ self-tapping screws that are screwed into clogged dowels, guide profiles are fixed;
- ✓ the ceiling profile is inserted into the guide profile and fixed with self-tapping screws;
- ✓ the vertically mounted profile is further strengthened by the suspension;
- ✓ on the frame. The drywall sheets are fastened with screws.

Important: In the instructions for aligning the walls in the bathroom you can find a recommendation for the use of wooden battens for the crate. Practice has shown that this cannot be done: over time they deteriorate, the profile must necessarily be metallic.

The second method of leveling the walls is plaster. To do this it is necessary that the walls are cleaned of the old finishes: tiles or paints (such an operation is not necessary in a new building), as well as from old plaster the cracks and holes must be filled as well as the masonry joints for better adhesion of the plaster to the wall and the surface is cleaned of grease, blackening and mold;

There is no fundamental difference in wall leveling technology depending on the material from which they are made, in modern buildings. An exception is the old brick houses, where the bathroom walls and plaster are made on a metal grid.

It is very difficult to remove the plaster layer, as there is a high probability of destroying the wall. Therefore, they resort to partial cleaning of exfoliated plaster.

If it was necessary to remove the grate and completely remove the plaster, the brick before plastering must be treated because of the increased humidity. If the walls are made of drywall or wood, they are easier to replace.

With independent work, nuances always emerge that can affect both the quality of work and the speed of their implementation.

✓ the walls under the plaster must be thoroughly cleaned. Any negligence can lead to the detachment of the plaster layer together with the tile;
✓ in order to prevent errors in the preparation of the solution, it is better to purchase ready-made mixtures, and when choosing a mixture, it is necessary to pay attention to which stage of the plastering work is planned, you cannot

experiment with the preparation of the solution - strictly follow the instructions;

In conclusion how to line the bathroom walls with tiles or paint is up to the owner. The right choice will allow for quality finishes.

To paint the walls are better aligned with drywall. At the same time, it can be put on glue or screwed to the crate with screws. For tiling the bathroom, plaster is more suitable - small errors will be removed with adhesive.

BATHROOM WITHOUT TILES: ADVANTAGES, IDEAS AND TIPS

Renovating the bathroom is no longer a complicated and monotonous operation dictated only by the need for maintenance and cleaning that this environment requires, but it is a way to renovate an important space in the house with original and creative choices.

The idea of abandoning the wall covering with tiles to color them thanks to resins and water-repellent paints goes exactly in this direction.

Bathroom surfaces are not only made to be covered with ceramic tiles, but also with materials such as resin, enamel, paint and lime putty.

The bathrooms without tiles are very cheap, but at the same time functional and practical if you take some precautions.

Let's see what they are!

These are original solutions, often cheaper and much faster, that guarantee maximum breathability of the walls and extreme hygiene. The results obtained are pleasing to the eye and adaptable to different furnishing styles.

Bathroom walls without tiles offer the advantage of more frequent changes, which are essential for cleaning and for the wear and tear to which this space is subject.

Covering a bathroom without tiles can solve the difficulty of finding the right match with wooden flooring.

Warm color varnishes can happily meet parquet, a very trendy choice for the bathroom, contrasted by many but which actually gives a modern and comfortable air to the environment.

On the other hand, when we have small walls or a blind bathroom, painting them with light shades can be an optimal solution to give brightness and give the illusion of an enlargement of the space.

The surface can be lightened by the use of color alone; in some cases, tiles with excessive decorations tend to further restrict already limited environments.

Light colors in the bathroom can be elegant and refined, as well as match the minimal modern style of a city apartment.

Use enamel in the bathroom without a coating

Another material suitable for filling the surfaces of the bathroom is the matte effect satin enamel which can create a pleasant effect both in a bathroom with a contemporary style and in a more classic one.

In this case, a combination of colors measured according to the chromatic scale is better to avoid unpleasant contrasts to the eye and out of place excesses.

For bathroom painting without tiles, we recommend that you avoid painting the wall at full height when the ceilings of your bathroom are of normal height, but it is preferable to find the "stop point", that is the point up to which to extend the color to then leave a white band on top of the colored wall.

A reference could be a shower tub with side glass, near which it is advisable to stop.

In larger spaces, coloring the surfaces can also allow you to exaggerate, sprinkling the same color on everything:

[161]

painting, in addition to the walls, also the ceiling and doors in the same tone can be very stylish and create an effect similar to that of a shell that wraps all the elements and furnishing accessories.

Bathroom coverings without tiles can also solve the problem of low ceilings.

Painting vertical lines across the height of the wall gives the illusion of soaring walls.

The width of the lines must be proportionate, so as to allow for a pleasant effect. To get it it is necessary to alternate two colors: a light one (usually white) and a darker one.

A classic combination is represented by white and gray, suitable both for a romantic or shabby chic style, and for a more refined and modern one.

This effect can also be recreated by covering the walls with wallpaper, used when you want to cover the bathroom without removing tiles.

If your bathroom has excellent natural light and has large windows or stained-glass windows, the use of paints on the walls can allow you to have no limits in the choice of shades and you can also dare with more intense colors.

Avoiding tiles does not mean preferring opaque surfaces, on the contrary the use of glossy enamel can give a strong brilliance to the environment.

Shimmering, smooth and vibrant walls can prove challenging, which is why it's best to limit them to one wall, leaving a more neutral breathable paint on the rest.

The enamel wall has the advantage of amplifying the space and can be a good idea when the bathroom is small or windowless.

If you have the opportunity to rely on an expert, the artistic resin can ensure you a much sought-after effect for your bathroom: a mix of colors that sprinkle the walls with shades.

Renovating a bathroom without removing the tiles is possible and can turn out to be an inexpensive and very quick way of renovating.

Deciding not to remove them can also be a choice of style and not necessarily an obligation linked to practical contingencies: if the format of the coverings is pleasant and the tiles are still in good condition, they can be repainted with a new color using a mini-roller to have a more homogeneous result.

The new touch of color will make the room appear as totally renovated, despite the minimal expenditure of energy.

Before starting the renovation, it is preferable to protect the sanitary ware and everything that must not be soiled.

You can choose a specific product, that is the tile enamel to be applied directly on the surface to be coated with only two coats.

Even adhesive, self-adhesive or thin stoneware tiles can allow you to cover the bathroom without removing the tiles; glued directly on the existing ones, they do not require intervention on the thickness of the doors when they are less than three mm.

The adhesive tiles are laid with the aid of a silicone glue, while the self-adhesive tiles already have an adhesive part on the back which facilitates the laying process on the old bathroom wall tiles even more.

In fact, they are very common in do-it-yourself renovations and adapt to different furnishing styles.

They do not place any limits on the choice of the surface you prefer, as they simulate many materials such as wood, ceramic, colored walls, reproduced with PVC or plastic, worked together with mineral details.

Composite materials, synthetic chemicals together with new technologies and advanced processing techniques have also improved their resistance.

BATHROOM WALL TILES: ALTERNATIVES FOR A BATHROOM WITHOUT TILES

Are you planning your new bathroom and are you interested in the most innovative trends? Do you want to renew the coverings in a modern way? Don't the usual tiles convince you? It can be done! Today, thanks to technical advances, materials are available that offer the same guarantees as traditional tiles in terms of waterproofing, but which guarantee a completely different aesthetic effect. Here are some cladding ideas for a bathroom without tiles, in a minimal style.

Bathroom coatings in synthetic enamel or water-repellent paint: low cost, maximum yield

A first option, inexpensive and with a pleasant visual impact, is the covering of the bathroom with synthetic enamel or water-repellent paint: unlike tiles, they do not require high installation costs. Furthermore, they do not present problems of laying or cutting, they respect hygienic standards and guarantee adequate resistance over time. In fact, water repellent paints counteract humidity and prevent the formation of mold.

Resin bathroom coverings: infinite decorative possibilities, identical resistance

For a qualitative leap from the decorative point of view, you can think of bathroom coatings in resin: the range of styles and colors satisfies every specific need, for a bathroom without tiles of exceptional aesthetic impact. The higher cost is compensated by the technical characteristics that ensure waterproofness, long-lasting resistance and hygiene.

Micro-cement: the last frontier of bathroom coverings

At a relatively low price it is possible to cover your bathroom without tiles with an innovative material, the result of a mixture of concrete and a special polymer. Micro-cement or micro-topping is ideal if you want to redesign the bathroom in a contemporary style, without sacrificing the technical characteristics of a material that adapts perfectly to any surface. Minimum thickness (3 mm), eco-friendly, resistant over time: what more could you ask for?

Bathroom cladding in wood, the alternative to painting that warms the environment

Wood floors and walls for the bathroom, why not? The treated wood is not afraid of wear and is resistant to humidity. Compared to water-based paints, it needs more maintenance, but transforms the bathroom into a welcoming and warm environment.

Bathroom wall tiles: which color to choose?

The bathroom without tiles requires special attention in the choice of color. Enamel, silicate or resin paint: a modern bathroom coating can be declined in a surprising variety of options and patterns. But beware: the visual impact and degree of illumination of such an important environment depend on the choice of shade.

The ideal look for all situations does not exist: space and light are elements to always keep in mind. Example: small or even blind bathroom without tiles? Avoid dark shades and go for neutral colors like gray. If, on the other hand, the bathroom is large and well-lit, you can dare darker paints, perhaps uneven or shaded. The possibilities are almost endless: bright colors, vertical striped solutions, multi-colored walls. And if after a few years you get tired, don't worry: changing color is very simple!

MOVING DRAINS - ALL THE THINGS YOU NEED TO KNOW

When completely renovating a home, rethinking the distribution of spaces, sometimes there is a need to reposition bathrooms and kitchens. To be sure of being able to carry out the project, first you need to check the feasibility of moving the drains to the desired position.

Moving a toilet even just a few meters can be problematic, therefore a thorough study of the positioning of the pipes is necessary. A fundamental step for a good functioning of the drains, which will allow you to have no problems. If you know everything there is to know about the subject, the idea of moving the bathroom will no longer seem so impossible!

How an exhaust system is made

All water (white, gray and black) must be conducted outside your home through pipes. In the first section, these are almost horizontal, with a slight (but very important) slope of at least 1%, which helps the liquids to flow without clogging the pipes. This means that, for every meter traveled by the pipes, there must be more than 1 cm of difference in inclination. The horizontal pipes lead the water to the vertical drainage columns, usually located near the toilet. Other components of the plumbing system are the vents, fittings and wells, which prevent the spread of bad smells.

Black waters, white waters and gray waters

The types of discharge are different depending on the type of water that must lead out of the house. The black water from the toilet flows into the vertical drain column and is dangerous for health due to the bacterial load it contains. On the contrary, the white waters are totally harmless and generally, channeled into a separate column. Then there are the gray waters, those that are discharged from sinks, bidets and showers, which need a simpler purification treatment than black ones.

Double-pipe or single-pipe systems?

In the double-pipe system, the discharges of black water and gray water are separated, precisely because they require different purification techniques. This system is an eco-sustainable option, as it requires more hygienic disposal, as there is no reflux of toilet water. In the single pipe system, common in condominiums, black water and gray water instead end up inside the same drain column. In more recent buildings or during a renovation, diversified water treatment plants can be inserted according to the type of discharge (septic tanks, degreasers and oil separators).

Small distances (less than a meter away)

Sometimes, during a renovation, the need arises to slightly shift the position of a drain. The reason may be due to the desire to create new partitions, or to redesign the internal configuration of the bathroom. If the movement is small, it can be quite simple to do. A specialized professional will always make sure to comply with all building regulations and ensure the proper functioning of the drains.

More consistent movements

When the renovations involve a new internal distribution with the displacement of services, or the addition of a second bathroom, the situation becomes complicated. Having verified the technical feasibility of the intervention, it is necessary to contact a technician who takes care of the bureaucratic procedures, communicating the start of the extraordinary renovation work.

WC with wall drain

When it is necessary to move the toilet, being able to carry out the intervention while keeping the drain on the ground can be complex, since it is always necessary to keep the correct slopes. To achieve this, the toilet and the floor are then raised by creating steps. Much easier in these cases, to opt for the installation of suspended sanitary ware, which use a wall drain, connected to the column through horizontal pipes. For this to be possible, however, a higher wall thickness (up to 20 cm) is required. If this is subtle, it is possible to intervene with the creation of a counter-wall, even if only for the portion where the sanitary fixtures are placed.

WC with wall drain

A decisive solution: the shredder

Would you like to make a second bathroom but think it is impossible to do it in your home? If the point where you want to build the services is not near the drain, there is still a solution. It involves the use of a shredder, inserted between the toilet and the pipes, which allows the use of pipes with a reduced diameter, even under 10 cm.

However, the shredder must be acoustically insulated through the use of sound-absorbing materials, in order to bring the noise produced below 35 decibels.

INSTALL A SINK IN 12 STEPS

There are sinks in many shapes, colors and materials. After choosing your sink you can start assembling it. The following instructions show you step by step how to do it, however a little experience is required.

Step 1 - Preparation before assembly: take measurements and close the central tap

Before purchasing, take all the measurements: total width of the sink, fixing distance, gap between drain and inflow, distance between floor and top corner of the countertop.

Remember: before starting the installation of the sink, empty the pipes and close the central tap. Also close the corner valves under the sink.

Step 2 - Unscrew the siphon and the tap from the old sink

First unscrew the siphon and the water drain hose. Collect the remaining water in a plastic basin. Finally, remove the connections to the taps under the sink and disassemble the taps.

Alternative: you can remove the tap even after you have removed the sink.

Step 3 - Remove the old sink

Remove the existing fixing screws and remove the sink. If the distance or fixing height of the new sink is no longer the same as before, remove all the fixing material: unscrew the old studs from the wall.

Step 4 - Drill the holes for the studs

If you need to drill holes in the tiles, first measure the height where to fix the new sink.

The height between the top edge of the sink should be approximately 85 cm. The drain should be in the center of the subsequent holes.

Make a sketch to make it easier to mount on the wall. Check the alignment of the holes with the help of the spirit level.

If you need to drill holes in the tiles, we recommend applying masking tape to prevent the drill from slipping off. Drill holes in the marked points using a tile drill bit. Never use a hammer drill. After drilling the tiles, use the drill again to drill the wall, being careful not to damage the tiles.

Then apply the appropriate plugs in the holes in the wall and check the stability.

Step 5 - Screw the studs to the wall

Screw the new studs with a wrench or pliers into the drilled holes until the metric thread protrudes from the wall.

Step 6 - Attach the tap to the sink

Insert the new tap into the holes in the new sink and screw it in from below. Tip: insert the fittings before assembling the sink and don't forget to insert all the gaskets.

(For taps, always observe the manufacturer's instructions!)

Step 7 - Secure the new sink

Hook the new sink to the protruding part of the screws so that it stays well supported.

To compensate for any unevenness in the wall and to avoid tensile stress, apply a strip of sealing mastic on the back, e.g. with sanitary silicone.

To do this, ask someone to help you push the sink onto the studs. Do not overtighten the fasteners, this way you can check the position of the sink with a spirit level and correct if necessary.

Make any position corrections, symmetrically and so as not to build up pressure. Finally, screw the correct retaining clips onto the ends of the studs.

Step 8 - Insulate the taps under the sink

Coat the threads of the new faucets under the sink with insulation paste and wrap it in hemp fabric. Alternatively, use a Teflon tape. Finally turn the taps upwards.

Step 9 - Connect the hoses to the taps under the sink

Insert the hose into the faucet under the sink and tighten the nuts for the fitting.

Step 10 - Insert the drain plug

Insert the drain plug into the sink opening. Hold the bottom of the valve by pushing it from below and then pull from above, then screw. Observe the manufacturer's instructions and assembly instructions.

Step 11 - Insert the drain hose and fit the drain kit

Insert the metal drain hose into the hole in the wall. To insulate, use a rubber sleeve. Then mount the exhaust equipment and the exhaust valve. Orient the opening of the siphon housing towards the wall. Fit and install the siphon holders. Also pay attention to the manufacturer's instructions.

Step 12 - Seal the space between the sink and the wall

Finally, seal the space between the sink and the wall with sanitary silicone. Observe the manufacturer's information and instructions. To spread the silicone, use a silicone scraper dipped in water and detergent.

Here is your new sink, installed quickly and easily. Turn on the water and check for leaks. Also check the gasket under the exhaust frame. Your new sink is not only practical and functional, it also gives that extra touch to your bathroom.

HOW TO REPLACE THE TOILET YOURSELF

The replacement of a bathroom fixture, in this case the toilet, can also be done by yourself and in this chapter we will explain how.

The first thing to bear in mind is that, nowadays, there are different types of sanitary ware, compared to the past, which also differ in terms of installation, position of drains, etc. Regarding the strengths and weaknesses of flush-to-wall, suspended or traditional floor-mounted sanitary ware, we have already written a specific article.

It is quite obvious that if we only want to change the toilet and are not instead intent on a complete makeover of the bathroom, with relative replacement of all the sanitary ware, we will have to use the same type of toilet previously installed and, possibly, the same model.

In our case it was not possible to recover a toilet identical to the old one (it was from 1966) and we therefore resorted to a Chinese model for a few dollars, bought in a department store, because it was our intention to have maximum savings since the new toilet fills the time span (which hopefully short) that separates us from the complete renovation of the bathroom and the expense of which, however, we could not face at this precise moment.

When you are in the conditions described above, therefore, you have to carefully evaluate what to do: if we have the possibility to immediately redo an old bathroom like the one shown in this article then let's do it; if, on the contrary, we cannot afford it, then we will only replace any broken sanitary ware, but we must be aware that the transition from one toilet model to another, even if apparently almost identical, involves many small and large inconveniences that we must be ready to solve.

[177]

Finally, if the bathroom is of recent construction but for some reason the toilet is broken then we must certainly recover the same type of model whose replacement will prove much easier since we do not have to make new fixing holes and any fittings for the drains.

In this case we will see how the toilet that was replaced was one of the most common with a floor drain; however, one is always impressed by the carelessness with which certain works were carried out in past years. The greatest difficulty encountered was related to the flushing water drain pipe which was bricked up and bent without further joints. In a case like this it would have been much better to also replace the drain pan but in order not to spend even one dollar more we used some remedies and left it in its place.

However, let's proceed in order and see the various steps to follow to change the toilet.

Disassemble the old toilet

Put on gloves before removing the toilet we assume that you have made some simple reflections, in light of the above considerations, regarding possible setbacks in the work.

Basically, we must evaluate how long it may take to complete all the work because if we do not have a second bathroom it could be embarrassing to have to ask the neighbors to host us in order to carry out our needs.

It took me about three hours (including breaks), alone, to replace the toilet. There are those who will be faster and those who will be slower. Everyone has to evaluate according to their abilities and it is better to expect two or three hours. In any case, to the actual time required for removal, cleaning and reinstallation, we must also add the time to go to the plumbing supplies store to buy what we need and, in general, what we need we learn with certainty only after we have disassembled the sanitary and made the bathroom partially and temporarily unusable.

Let's get to the point: close the water valve located near the toilet cistern (if we are not sure we close the general valve) and let's wear gloves that are hygienic. In my case I used latex gloves even if they are not ideal for this kind of work; certainly, allow maximum sensitivity to the hands.

The toilet siphon contains a certain amount of water that should be removed before proceeding to remove the toilet; you can do this by soaking old rags or using a wet vacuum cleaner if you have one. In any case, it is not strictly necessary to remove the water as if you do not overturn the jar it should remain inside the siphon. It is certainly better to flush the toilet a few times to make sure that the water in it is as clean as possible.

In my case the problem did not arise as the reason I was forced to change the vase was due to a series of cracks in the ceramic that made the water disperse on the floor.

Remember that once the water valve is closed, it is advisable to flush the toilet to have the cistern empty during the disassembly operations.

The removal of the vessel is relatively simple.

First of all, we remove the toilet seat which constitutes a footprint during all operations.

It is then a question of removing the fixing screws that anchor the toilet to the floor, cutting off the silicone that sealed the toilet to the floor and then removing the seal gasket of the water tank drain from its seat.

To cut the silicone we use a very sharp cutter. We pay attention because in the really old and never renovated bathrooms the sanitary ware may have been fixed with white cement instead of silicone; in this case the operations become a little more difficult and there is the risk of breaking even the vessel in an attempt to remove it.

Once all the accessory elements have been removed, we should end up with only the vase resting on the ground. At this point we try, with caution, to make it detach from the silicone bead that may have remained by lifting it with small lateral movements until we feel it yield and rise; at that point it is necessary to remove, always with a certain delicacy, the toilet from the sling and from the drain pipe of the cistern.

A new toilet and other materials

Now that we have removed the old toilet it is a matter of taking some measures and preparing everything necessary to be able to place the new toilet.

As you can see in the photos in this article, there is always some silicone sticking to the floor once the toilet is removed. I will not describe here the operations to be carried out to clean the floor from the old hardened silicone as we have dedicated a specific article to it that I invite you to read.

It will also be necessary to remove the old plugs if, in all likelihood, the fixing holes of the new vase do not have an identical distance to those of the previous one. To remove the plugs, we use a pair of pliers; it is a tiring operation because when it comes to screwing them, we do it by turning the nut but when it comes to removing them there is only one screw without a nut which is a bit difficult to turn.

Once we have brought the new toilet home (let's handle it with care because it is easy to chip the ceramic), place it near its final location and evaluate if the distances between the various elements match or if there are additional works to be carried out.

In my case I immediately noticed that the distance between the fixing plugs was not identical (the old vase had a distance between the plugs of 16 centimeters while the new one of 18 centimeters), but this was estimated; what is worse is that the rear inlet hole of the toilet cistern's drain hose was slightly higher. What to do in this case? As already said the best thing was to buy a new cistern with an external tube that would also have facilitated the assembly of the pot; I adopted a buffer solution by heating the plastic tube with the flame, until it softened slightly, until it entered the rear hole. I repeat that this is not the ideal solution, but only the cheapest.

It was also immediately evident that a connection gasket was needed between the toilet drain and the floor sling. No gasket was even installed on the old toilet because the ceramic part of the toilet entered directly into the drain sling. With the new vase it was therefore necessary to adopt this sort of connection extension which, being eccentric, will allow even small movements of the vase to be better managed compared to the original position.

Fit the new toilet

We are almost ready to fit the new toilet, but we still have to test and place the seals first. We have already said about the eccentric gasket; you will also need to purchase a rubber gasket for the inlet of the cassette drain hose.

The seals of the toilet

The eccentric seal is generally quite long and, nine times out of ten, needs to be cut. Manufacturers foresee this possibility and in fact there is a cutting line to shorten the gasket when necessary. To cut the gasket we can use a sharp cutter (be careful, especially when we put it in the plastic) which will allow you to remove the excess part. Once we have cut the eccentric gasket, all we have to do is insert it completely on the ceramic drain of the toilet.

The fixing dowels

Now comes the perhaps most difficult part. We saw how the old dowels could not be used to fix the new toilet. To calculate precisely the position in which we will have to drill the holes, therefore, we just have to position the toilet in the final position and then mark the exact position where to make the holes with a permanent marker.

At this point we remove the toilet once more and, using a drill with a suitable tip, we make the holes in correspondence with the marker marks, taking care to make holes as perpendicular to the floor as possible.

As you can see from the images, if you buy the dowels of certain brands, many useful indications are specified on the package such as the size of the drill bit to use and the depth of the hole to be made.

Once we have made the holes, we vacuum all the dust and, if necessary, clean the floor with denatured alcohol, in order to make the surface perfectly suitable to accommodate the silicone bead that we will apply later.

In this regard, we remind you that the silicone should be put on the lower part of the toilet where it comes into contact with the floor and only after that the toilet should be placed in position. For reasons related to the drain pipe of the walled toilet bowl it was not possible, in this case, to apply the silicone first, as to fit the toilet on the pipe it was necessary to perform a few maneuvers with the consequence that we would only have muddied the floor. In my case, I put the silicone on afterwards, once the toilet was completely fixed. As you can see, there is no unique way to carry out certain jobs, you must always be flexible and able to adapt to circumstances, including overcoming the "rules" if necessary.

The definitive fixation

We have reached the last part of the work.

Once the toilet has been correctly positioned on the drain sling, by means of the eccentric gasket, and the pipe of the toilet cistern has entered the rear hole of the toilet, we will only have to fix the toilet to the floor definitively.

We tighten the screw and the nut as shown in the following images, but before tightening them fully we check again if the vessel is level using the level; if necessary, it may be necessary to insert plastic wedges under the toilet to bring it level.

Now we can tighten the nuts completely until the pot is firm and stable. The subsequent operations are almost of a simple routine compared to what has been done up to now; we carefully fix the gasket of the pipe of the cistern to the toilet and reposition the seat.

Now it's time for tests and checks! We reopen the water valve, wait for the water tank to fill up and flush the toilet. If everything works right, we shouldn't see any water leaks. In my case, a small addition of silicone was required to remedy a small leak from the rear seal that should seal the cistern tube to the toilet.

THE 5 THINGS TO KNOW BEFORE CHOOSING BATHROOM FIXTURES

Of all the bathroom elements, the sanitary fixtures seem to be the least important: if you believe that, it is only because you have always been lucky in your choice! In fact, if you make the wrong choices, you will understand that there is nothing worse than an uncomfortable and not very functional toilet. I have collected in this post the 6 things to consider before choosing a sanitary:

1. Choose the rimless toilet

We are used to seeing the toilet with that very thick inner ceramic edge from which the water comes out. It is ugly, uncomfortable and difficult to clean. For some years now there has been the solution: rimless sanitary ware. More beautiful, quieter and easier to clean. There are only advantages to choosing this type of toilet.

2. Easy to clean toilet? No problem

Admit it, when you read "easy to clean" in the previous point, your eyes lit up. Well, get used to so many other comforts. First of all, because various manufacturers integrate titanium dioxide in the enamel layer, which naturally fights bacterial proliferation: no commitment is required on your part, your toilet will take care of not reproducing E. coli and many other bacteria! Toilet seat covers have also become extremely convenient for cleaning - many companies make them easily removable, which means you won't need to use the Allen key to be able to remove the toilet seat from the toilet itself. Some companies produce a convenient button to press to be able to remove it, others even without any mechanism: just pull upwards to release the toilet seat. Finally, easy to clean toilets!

3. In addition,

25% of the water we use during the day is used to rinse the toilet. For this reason, since 2014 the European Union has tried to encourage water saving in this sector by creating a water saving label. You know when you buy a new chandelier or a TV, which always has a label that perhaps shows the letter "A" to make you understand that it will consume little power? The sanitary ware has the European Water Label, a label that shows in black and white how many liters the sanitary ware needs for rinsing. At the time of the creation of the label the goal was to reach 3 liters and... guess what? We got there. Why this saving of liters is so important I can show you by making a quick calculation. Let's assume in an average family to use the toilet 20 times a day: we do the calculations with 3 possible different drains (9, 6 and 3 liters).

- ✓ 20 x 9 l = 180 liters / day x 365 = 65,700 liters / year
- ✓ 20 x 6 l = 120 liters / day x 365 = 43,800 liters / year
- ✓ 20 x 3 l = 60 liters / day x 365 = 21.900 liters / year

There are 26 million families in Italy alone. If we all went from discharging 9 liters to just 3 liters it would mean saving almost 570 billion cubic meters of water. Five hundred and seventy billion cubic meters!

4. Raw materials and glazing

Those who read me habitually know I am a great supporter of 'Made in Italy'. Relying on Italian manufacturing companies guarantees to have high quality standards, both in the selection of raw materials and in the manufacturing processes. The world of sanitary ware nowadays has a strong price division between Italian production and foreign production: the latter often costs much less to the end customer, just go around some online store to get an idea. If you are looking at an imported product, try to find out some information about the manufacturer (which is not necessarily the company that offers the item in its catalog, since some collections are only marketed!) To make sure of the quality of the product.

5. Choose a comfortable size

Hardly anyone has the giant bathrooms you see in magazines and photographs, we agree, so every inch recovered in the bathroom is worth gold. However, choosing bathroom fixtures with a small size becomes really uncomfortable and is therefore not recommended in all cases where it can be done without. The normal depth of the bathroom fixtures is usually 53 centimeters: the most "important" models even reach up to almost 60 centimeters. If you can, don't go below the standard. In fact, there are all the reduced sizes, which even reach up to 45 cm in depth, which allow you to save centimeters at the expense of comfort.

TOILET BOWL SELECTION GUIDE: HOW TO CHOOSE THE PERFECT TOILET BOWL FOR THE BATHROOM

Design the bathroom. Renovate the bathroom. Furnish the bathroom. The bathroom has priority because it is the heart of the house of our dreams, as well as the environment that characterizes it most strongly, the room in which the combination of aesthetic and functional needs must be maximum. Yes, but when we talk about bathroom furniture, which elements do we focus on most? Shower cubicles, mirrors, coverings, lighting. More rarely, our attention is directed to other components, which are only superficially considered marginal. The toilet, for example. Is one worth more than the other? Error.

Which type of toilet to choose?

The choice of the toilet is important and oriented by a preliminary choice of field. The ideal situation is that it happens during the renovation phase, when it is still possible to decide where to place the drains. If, on the other hand, it is a question of replacing sanitary ware already in use, it is possible that the options are reduced precisely in relation to the necessary work.

In general, the assessments to be made are practical, hygienic and - why not? - aesthetics. There are three types of toilet to consider: the traditional toilet, the flush-to-the-wall toilet and the suspended toilet.

Traditional toilet: the toilet with pedestal and drain fixed to the floor. Classic, widespread in the white ceramic version, easy to install, stable in terms of morphology and economical. Flaws? Difficult to clean in the space that is created between the toilet and the wall, cluttered and, since the eye also wants its part, it is not exactly the best of life

Flush-to-wall toilet: as in the traditional option, this is a toilet with floor drain. The fundamental difference, which improves the visual impact and makes cleaning operations easier, consists in the almost total absence of space between the toilet and the wall. No exposed pipes or external fittings. However, it is necessary to pay more attention to the assembly phase.

Wall hung toilet: wall drain for a modern design toilet. It is no coincidence that it is the solution that is popular today: beyond the intrinsic elegance, a suspended sanitary toilet is more hygienic because it facilitates the cleaning of the surrounding environment, takes up less space, does not transmit acoustic vibrations to the floor, does not suffer from the typical wear of silicone joints found in traditional toilets. What does it need? The wall drain cannot be separated from a minimum wall thickness of 12 cm, net of tiles and plaster. If not installed perfectly, it can be less stable.

Rimless toilet: for a surplus of hygiene, acoustic comfort and functionality

For some time now, all the companies in the sector have patented modern toilet models with a singular and intelligent feature: they are rimless toilets, that is, without the curved edge from which the drainage water flows. The rim is difficult to clean and can become a breeding ground for germs and limescale. For this reason, the rimless toilet, in which the flow of water is conveyed along special grooves along the perimeter of the toilet, represents a hygienic and easily cleanable alternative. The rimless toilet is also quieter.

Washlet: The Japanese toilet that takes us into the future

The toilet of the future comes from Japan and has already forcefully entered our market: it is called washlet and combines the functions of the toilet and bidet in a single sanitary vessel. How? Thanks to a nozzle suitably addressed and managed with a special multi-function push-button panel.

The water jet is not the only feature of the washlets, futuristic technological jewels that can be customized with a multitude of options: dryer, jet and seat temperature regulator, automatic flush and lid opening, sound effects. The Japanese toilet is truly the last frontier of bathroom furniture, destined to revolutionize the market.

BATHROOM ACCESSORIES: WHICH ONES TO CHOOSE AND USEFUL TIPS TO AVOID MAKING MISTAKES.

They are called accessories, but they are fundamental elements in bathroom furnishings, they not only complete the aesthetics of an environment, but make it practical and functional.

The latest trends offer bathroom accessories with minimal lines, often compact and multi-use.

However, companies satisfy all tastes, with a wide range of bathroom accessories, accessories, mirrors and containers.

Sometimes they are part of the sanitaryware collections, but the beauty is to feel free to mix, experiment with new combinations and take advantage of the versatility of each object.

But how to choose bathroom accessories? Some useful tips to avoid making mistakes.

Space is the element to be evaluated at the outset, not only because "taking measurements" is a must, but also because the bathroom is one of the most used rooms and the space must necessarily be optimized.

In larger rooms, accessories are used to furnish, to make them even more welcoming and pleasant.

To be considered together with the space is functionality.

As obvious as it is that bathroom accessories must be functional, it cannot be taken for granted that they actually are. In fact, various factors come into play: such as the materials, the shapes, the installation.

The perfect bathroom accessories fulfil their function and multiply the possibilities of use.

Wall-mounted bathroom accessories are indispensable for small rooms because they allow you to take advantage of every surface… even the vertical ones.

Soap holders are also shelving and shelves become towel holders!

The roll holders installed on the wall can also be used as magazine holders.

Larger rooms, lived in by the whole family, can be furnished with practical and versatile accessories.

The stools can also be used as magazine racks or towel racks (for those who want to keep the sponges in sight!).

More and more often the traditional "toilet brushes", in the free-standing version, also house the roll holder or the towel holder.

Free-standing towel racks are real furnishing elements.

Hygiene.

In the bathroom, hygiene is essential and in the choice of bathroom accessories it is better to prefer shapes and materials that allow you to sanitize easily, frequently and in depth, avoiding bad odors and the formation of unpleasant molds.

This mainly applies to toothbrush holders, soap holders and the toilet brush where water stagnation is created.

Shopping.

The budget factor is essential. The range of possibilities is now almost infinite because there are so many manufacturing companies.

But be careful because often evaluating only the cost of the objects you forget about all the other important factors.

Poor quality bathroom accessories can easily deteriorate in contact with water, but also favor the reproduction of molds.

Style.

You can indulge in this, there are no rules. "Neutral" style accessories are often preferred, perhaps in polished or brushed steel with traditional shapes, but more and more frequently it is preferred to completely break with the style and furnishings of the bathroom by choosing bright colors, innovative materials and shapes.

A separate chapter concerns mirrors, bathroom accessories essential for their function, but also for versatility.

The right installation of the mirrors makes it possible to make an environment optically larger and if combined with the right lighting they become indispensable elements.

Precision lights or backlights, the possibilities are different.

Then there are the container mirrors, allies of small spaces. To be evaluated in the presence of countertop washbasins on shelves, but also to multiply the usable space with a practically invisible solution.

CONCLUSION

Designing the bathroom well is the first step.

The errors that you will find below are often the result of "improvised" restructuring interventions in which mistakes can be made that cannot be remedied, if not at significant costs.

And often the error is initial because we rely on a "little project", little thought, fast and approximate.

The bathroom project will reshape your space and involve the bathroom as a whole, therefore the ceiling, walls, lights, floors and furniture elements with the aim of reorganizing the spaces according to functionality and aesthetics. Studying the space trying to avoid mistakes due to improvisation or do-it-yourself is essential.

1st error:

Just redo the "face" of the bathroom

When renovating a bathroom that is already 25/30 years old, it is also worth redoing all the pipes, not just the floors and walls.

If you are interested in changing only the bathroom tiles, then you can find many indications in this chapter that we have dedicated to this specific topic.

If, on the other hand, you listen to the advice to also redo the bathroom systems, then the technology you should use for the pipes is that of multilayer pipes.

The multilayer pipe looks like a continuous pipe. There are no fittings, elbows or other special pieces to weld to the pipe.

This will allow you to avoid having "under-track critical points" and possible breakages and consequent losses.

2nd error:

Decide the position of the sanitary fixtures / shower / sink without taking into account the distance from the drain column.

The location of the drain column is the first thing to know when tackling a bathroom renovation. This is because the position of the toilet cannot be decided without considering that the drain pipe generally has a diameter of 11 cm and will run on the floor, under the screed, up to the drain column with a slope of at least 1 cm per linear meter, to ensure proper operation.

This minimum slope, combined with the available thickness between the floor and the finished floor, gives us a constraint on the maximum distance between the drain column and the position of the toilet.

We have to do the same attention and reasoning for the shower.

A flush-to-floor shower tray is increasingly being created. In order to achieve this, the space available under the floor must be checked to ensure the slope of the drain up to the column. If there is little thickness, a flush-to-floor plate cannot be created, otherwise the water would not flow correctly into the drain column.

If there are no slopes - as they say in the jargon - we will be condemned to put the highest shower tray and create a step (very uncomfortable as well as ugly)

3rd error:

Purchase the suspended sanitary ware without having checked the thickness of the wall on which they will be mounted

A load-bearing wall is not needed to mount the suspended sanitary ware, but it is not a good idea if the wall is built with the classic 8 cm perforated brick or, worse, in an unreinforced plasterboard wall, a 12 cm brick is the condition minimal.

So, if you are building your new home, remember to consider these details well in advance as well. If you are renovating and you do not want or cannot redo the walls of the room, the first thing to do is to investigate to understand how the walls you have available are made.

4th error:

Purchase floor-standing sanitary ware flush with the wall instead of the classic ones detached from the wall without having checked the compatibility of the connections

To renew the style of a fairly recent bathroom, which on the whole still likes it, it is sometimes enough to install new sanitary ware.

Often you only want to replace the bathroom fixtures, to make the bathroom more modern and practical, by removing the old model detached from the walls to mount the new model flush with the wall, it seems so easy... easier said than done!

It is true that there are models that are created precisely for this purpose, they have the "translated exhaust" or the "universal exhaust", but they are not always compatible.

The hot and cold-water connections of the bidet can be so far apart that no back-to-wall bidet could be installed without breaking the tiles and moving them. The flushing of the toilet may be too high or too low even for the toilet with a sliding drain.

5th error:

Thinking that all sanitary ware is compatible. There are no "standard arrangements"!

Each model of sanitary ware has a precise technical data sheet that indicates how to prepare the connections, at what heights and how to prepare the brackets (in the case of the suspended).

Remember that a model must always be chosen before making the implants. If the plumber has prepared the connections without asking you which sanitary fixtures you intend to install, it means that ... he has chosen for you!

6th error:

Let the plumber assemble the concealed parts of the mixers of his choice, and you will no longer be able to choose the model you like!

What has been said in point 5 also applies to mixers in a similar way: there is no "standard built-in part" as I sometimes hear.

Each tap manufacturer uses its own built-in parts. Choosing to mount the fitting of a particular company means "marrying" that company and then both the external parts and the rest of the taps of that specific company will have to be ordered.

7th error:

Forget to apply the waterproofing membrane in the shower area before laying the tiles

The tile does not let water through but the joint could be a weak point and the water could seep in and create damp spots on the other side of the wall.

Before laying the tiles, the installer himself spreads a liquid membrane with a spatula both on the masonry walls and on the plasterboard.

8th error:

Order the shower cubicle before having installed the shower tray and coverings

The most beautiful shower stalls are those with a minimal frame, they are the easiest to clean but they are also the ones that hold less water (I remind you that the shower is not an aquarium, so the boxes are not "watertight"!).

Less frame also means less possibility of adjustment during the assembly phase and therefore the measures to order the shower box must be taken after the plate has been laid (sometimes the plumber casts it slightly under the plaster) and when the coverings are completed.

Of course, you will have to accept that the bathroom is incomplete and wait for the box, but only then will you be sure that it will be perfect. In fact, there are 3 mm thin tiles and even more than 2 cm thick marble tiles, so the size of the box can change a lot.

If, for example, you buy a 100x80 plate, let's assume that it is placed against the walls without embedding it.

Then a 12 mm thick tile covering is laid (with the glue we get to about 15 mm).

At the end of the work, the shower tray will measure approximately 98.5x78.5.

Here, this is the useful size to order the shower enclosure, not the initial 100x80!

9th error:

Don't study lighting

Light makes a difference, always. Especially in the bathroom. We can think of light with the sole function of illuminating, or of light with the function of relaxing or reactivating (RGB lights in a shower) or even with the function of furnishing (backlighting of a mirror, effect lights around a bathtub, pendant lights that drop from the ceiling).

10th error:

Don't forget the rest of the house

The bathroom is not a world apart!

It is part of the entire house and must consistently follow its style. Entering a bathroom and feeling catapulted into another world is really annoying, so watch out for your choices!

BATHROOM REMODELING - Amy Landry

www.ingramcontent.com/pod-product-compliance
Lightning Source LLC
Chambersburg PA
CBHW061153120626
46546CB00005B/2050